Oriens

ORIENS

A PILGRIMAGE THROUGH ADVENT AND CHRISTMAS

December 1, 2024–February 2, 2025

FR. JOEL SEMBER

Our Sunday Visitor
Huntington, Indiana

Nihil Obstat
Msgr. Michael Heintz, Ph.D.
Censor Librorum

Imprimatur
Kevin C. Rhoades
Bishop of Fort Wayne-South Bend
February 9, 2024

The *Nihil Obstat* and *Imprimatur* are official declarations that a book is free from doctrinal or moral error. It is not implied that those who have granted the *Nihil Obstat* and *Imprimatur* agree with the contents, opinions, or statements expressed.

Our Sunday Visitor Publishing Division
Our Sunday Visitor, Inc.
200 Noll Plaza
Huntington, IN 46750
1-800-348-2440

ISBN: 978-1-63966-212-8 (Inventory No. T2902)
1. RELIGION—Holidays—Christmas & Advent.
2. RELIGION—Christian Living—Prayer.
3. RELIGION—Christianity—Catholic.
eISBN: 978-1-63966-213-5

Cover design: Tyler Ottinger
Interior design: Amanda Falk
Cover and interior art: Adobestock

PRINTED IN THE UNITED STATES OF AMERICA

*Dedicated to St. Kateri Tekakwitha, Lily of the Mohawks,
lover of poverty and chastity, and servant of the sick and elderly*

+

*and to Fr. Paul Timmerman, fellow traveler on
the journey to healing and wholeness*

+

*and to the parish staff of the Antigo Area Catholic
Churches, who have become like a family to me*

+

¡Buen Camino!

WEEK 1
Sunday, December 1
ADVENT, 1ST SUNDAY

Friday, December 6 — SAINT NICHOLAS

WEEK 2
Sunday, December 8
ADVENT, 2ND SUNDAY

Monday, December 9 — IMMACULATE CONCEPTION

Thursday, December 12 — OUR LADY OF GUADALUPE

WEEK 3
Sunday, December 15
ADVENT, 3RD SUNDAY

WEEK 4
Sunday, December 22
ADVENT, 4TH SUNDAY

Wednesday, December 25 — NATIVITY OF OUR LORD

WEEK 5
Sunday, December 29
HOLY FAMILY

Wednesday, January 1 — MARY, MOTHER OF GOD

WEEK 6
Sunday, January 5
EPIPHANY, OBSERVED

Monday, January 6 — EPIPHANY

Sunday, January 12 — BAPTISM OF THE LORD

WEEK 7
Sunday, January 12
BAPTISM OF THE LORD

WEEK 8
Sunday, January 19
ORDINARY TIME, 2ND SUNDAY

WEEK 9
Sunday, January 26
ORDINARY TIME, 3RD SUNDAY

Sunday, February 2 — THE PRESENTATION OF THE LORD

WEEK 10
Sunday, February 2
THE PRESENTATION OF THE
LORD

Contents

Introduction

Give a man a fish, and you feed him for a day.
Teach a man to pray, and you feed him for a lifetime.

TEACH A MAN TO PRAY …

There are many wonderful Advent books full of moving meditations for you to choose from. This isn't one of them. Instead of giving you meditations I came up with, *Oriens* (pronounced OR-ee-ens, like Orient and Oreo cookie) will teach you how to meditate for yourself. If you don't really know how to pray with Scripture, this book will teach you. If you already know how to pray, then it will help you to pray better. I left space each day for you to journal your prayer experiences. When you get to the end of the book, you will find that it is full of moving meditations, but they won't be my meditations; they'll be yours. I hope that, as you learn to go deeper in your conversations with God, prayer becomes your favorite part of each day, and this season takes on a whole new meaning.

IF YOU HAVE PRAYED WITH *ORIENS* BEFORE

You might be wondering how this book compares to previous editions. The format is exactly the same: We teach *lectio divina* and imaginative prayer and provide a Scripture passage each day. We also give you space to journal. You will encounter familiar figures like John the Baptist, Zechariah, and, of course, Mary and Joseph. Much of the material in this book was first released in the 2021 edition. The dates, days of the week, and feast days have been adjusted to match the date of Christmas. There are also new Scripture passages that have not appeared in *Oriens* before. Some of the meditations have been updated, and there is some new explanatory material. The countdown to Christmas and a few feast days like the Holy Innocents are the same every year. *Oriens* 2024 will be like walking down a familiar road, but with new companions and at a new place in your life. If you've never done *Oriens* before, finish reading the introduction and then skim the rest of the introductory material through the first day (Sunday, December 1). That will give you a good sense of the road ahead.

"DO YOU WANT TO WALK THE CAMINO WITH ME?"

It was my third year of theology at the North American College in Rome. We had two weeks of Easter vacation to go experience Europe. A classmate and I decided to walk the Camino Portugués, a shorter version of the famous medieval pilgrimage route across Spain. (It's so famous that it's called simply *El Camino*, which means "The Way" in Spanish.) I bought some shoes and borrowed a backpack, and we flew to Lisbon. We took a train to the Portuguese border and spent a week walking to the burial place of St. James the apostle. Something special happened on the way. I started to see myself, and the ordinary world, in a whole new way. I discovered the magic of walking pilgrimages.

Three years later I was back in America as a newly ordained priest. "We don't have to fly to Europe to walk down the road," I thought. I scoped out a walking route to a local shrine, lined up places to stay every twelve miles or so, and found people to bring us food each night. Twenty-two people joined me on that pilgrimage. Their lives were changed, and I realized that the magic of walking pilgrimages isn't limited to the plains of Spain. Every year for the past ten years, I've led a five-day walking pilgrimage to the Shrine of Our Lady of Good Help in Champion, Wisconsin. I never cease to come away with some new gift, blessing, or lesson learned on the way.

Walking pilgrimages are a much different experience from a bus pilgrimage. When you ride a bus to a shrine, it's mostly about the destination. Pilgrims look forward to a big "Aha" moment waiting for them when they arrive. Walking pilgrims, on the other hand, learn the joy of the journey. They see familiar roads in a whole new way. They appreciate the beauty around them. They enter into the ebb and flow of nature. They draw closer to the people they walk with. They learn to keep their eyes open for encounters with God along the way. Most of all, they learn to put one foot in front of the other and keep walking no matter what. A walking pilgrimage is about more than the destination; it's a journey of the heart. It changes you in ways that you never expected.

THE ADVENT JOURNEY

So, what does this have to do with Advent and Christmas? We all struggle with Advent. The Church is telling us to slow down, but the world is telling us, "Hurry up." We rush around preparing for the birth of Jesus. We look forward to the big "Aha" moment waiting for us at Christmas. And we always seem to miss out somehow. How is it that every year Christmas seems less merry and bright than we were hoping it would be? Too often, Christmas seems to fly by even more quickly than Advent does!

The problem is that we keep treating Advent like the bus on the way to Christmas. We expect to step off at Bethlehem and have some kind of amazing experience. I believe Holy Mother Church designed Advent to be more like a walking pilgrimage. You take a little step every day. You learn to enjoy the journey instead of rushing to Christmas — and then you're better prepared to enjoy the full Christmas season, rather than rushing to get the celebration over with. You connect with the people around you. You enter into a new rhythm. The ordinary things of life start to take on a new meaning. God meets you on the road. Think of this book as a Camino guidebook. It will show you how to step off the busy Christmas bus and walk the Advent road one day at a time. You will learn that Advent and Christmas are more than destinations; they involve a journey of the heart.

KEEP WALKING

This book covers nearly ten weeks, from the first Sunday of Advent on December 1 to the feast of the Presentation on February 2. The feast of the Presentation (also called Candlemas) is the traditional final day after which Christmas decorations must be taken down. That way you will get almost four weeks to prepare for Christmas and forty days to celebrate Christmas (kind of like the forty days of Lent followed by the fifty days of Easter). We need those extra days. None of the people who saw the Christ Child in person understood the true meaning of Christmas. It was only in the days and years afterward that the "dawn from on high" began to rise in their hearts (see Lk 1:78). The same is true for us in our ongoing journey of faith. Praying with this devotional until February 2 will help you continue to see Jesus in the ordinary. Besides, it's easier to pray in the post-Christmas lull, and we need a little help getting through the low time in January.

You don't have to walk the whole way with me; it's your journey and you can quit any time. But let me encourage you to plan for a longer walk. Consider putting up your Christmas tree a little later this year. Put on the lights and ornaments, but don't plug in the lights until the Light of the World is born on December 25. Then keep your tree lit all through the twelve days until January 6. Plan to keep at least your Advent wreath and Nativity scene up until February 2. It may seem like a long way to go now, but you'll be surprised at how quickly it passes. And you'll really enjoy those extra days.

IF YOU MISS A DAY

Even when you are too busy to pray, try to at least open this book and read the Scripture passage each day. If you end up missing a day or two (or even a week), don't try to go back and do all the meditations you missed. Just skip ahead to the current day and pray that one well. It is not important that you do every single meditation; what matters is that you put your heart into your prayer. Prayer is experiencing how God our Father looks at you with love. Holiness is learning to live in his long, loving gaze every moment of your life.

You might assume that because I wrote this book that I'm great at praying. Far from it! I was trained as a spiritual director through the Institute for Priestly Formation. I have taught countless numbers of people how to pray. I've been on pilgrimages and retreats and even a thirty-day silent retreat. But the truth is, unless I'm actually on a retreat or a pilgrimage, I usually pray badly. Most days I'm too busy, distracted, self-absorbed, or lazy to really pray well. And the problem is compounded during the busy Advent and Christmas season. I wrote this book because I need it too! I will be praying with you and for you this whole season. Please pray for me and for your fellow *Oriens* pilgrims. We each make our own journey, and every journey is unique, but no one walks alone. *¡Buen Camino!*

Fr. Joel Sember
Priest, Pastor, Pilgrim

Suggested Calendar for the Advent and Christmas Season

December 1, 1st Sunday of Advent: Light the first candle on your Advent wreath.

December 6 (Friday): Give some treats for Saint Nicholas Day.

December 8, 2nd Sunday of Advent: Light the second candle on your Advent wreath. Put up your crèche (manger scene).

December 15, 3rd Sunday of Advent: Light the third (rose) candle on your Advent wreath.

Sometime this week: Put up your Christmas tree. Decorate it, but don't plug the lights in. Wait until the Light of the World is born.

December 22, 4th Sunday of Advent: Light the fourth candle on your Advent wreath.

December 24/25: After attending Christmas Mass, put the Baby Jesus in the crèche and light up your Christmas tree. Change the candles in your Advent wreath to white.

January 1 (Wednesday): Octave Day of Christmas, solemnity of Mary, Mother of God. Start the new year with Mary.

January 5 (Sunday) or 6 (Monday): Epiphany. Have a family party to bless your home with blessed chalk. Afterward you can take down the tree (if you want to) and the decorations, but don't take down the Advent wreath or the crèche.

February 2 (Sunday): Feast of the Presentation. Have one last Christmas party! Light the candles on your wreath and have a family Candlemas procession to the crèche. Sing Christmas carols. Then put away all remaining Christmas decorations.

Blessing of an Advent Wreath

The use of the Advent Wreath is a traditional practice which has found its place in the Church as well as in the home. The blessing of an Advent Wreath takes place on the First Sunday of Advent or on the evening before the First Sunday of Advent. When the blessing of the Advent Wreath is celebrated in the home, it is appropriate that it be led by the father (if present) or the eldest/senior member of the household.

All make the Sign of the Cross together: + In the Name of the Father, and of the Son, and of the Holy Spirit.
Leader: Our help is in the name of the Lord.
Response: Who made heaven and earth.
A reading from the Book of the Prophet Isaiah:

> The people who walked in darkness
>   have seen a great light;
> Upon those who lived in a land of gloom
>   a light has shone.
> You have brought them abundant joy
>   and great rejoicing;
> They rejoice before you as people rejoice at harvest,
>   as they exult when dividing the spoils.
> For a child is born to us, a son is given to us;
>   upon his shoulder dominion rests.
> They name him Wonder-Counselor, God-Hero,
>   Father-Forever, Prince of Peace.
> His dominion is vast
>   and forever peaceful,
> Upon David's throne, and over his kingdom,
>   which he confirms and sustains
>   by judgment and justice,
>   both now and forever. (Isaiah 9:1–2, 5–6)

Leader: The word of the Lord.
Response: Thanks be to God.
Leader: Let us pray.

> Lord our God, we praise you for your Son, Jesus Christ: He is Emmanuel, the hope of the peoples, he is the wisdom that teaches and guides us, he is the Savior of every nation.

> Lord God, let your blessing come upon us as we light the candles of this wreath. May the wreath and its light be a sign of Christ's promise to bring us salvation. May he come quickly and not delay. We ask this through Christ our Lord.

Response: Amen.

The blessing may conclude with a verse from "O Come, O Come, Emmanuel":

> O come, desire of nations, bind
> in one the hearts of humankind
> bid ev'ry sad division cease
> and be thyself our Prince of peace.
> Rejoice! Rejoice! Emmanuel
> shall come to thee, O Israel.
>   — From *Catholic Household Blessings & Prayers*

Week One

Lectio Divina

This first week we will use an ancient prayer form called *lectio divina* (pronounced "LEK-si-o di-VEE-na"). It has four simple steps, known by their Latin names: *lectio* (reading), *meditatio* (meditation), *oratio* (prayer), and *contemplatio* (contemplation). Don't worry about each Latin word. The prayer form is as simple as this: Read, Think, Talk, Listen.

We read a passage of Scripture and lots of thoughts come to our mind: What does this word mean? What is the cultural and historical context? How have scholars interpreted this particular idea? Those aren't bad things to research. Some of those questions can form the *meditatio* part of the prayer. But we need to avoid getting stuck in our own heads. Reading Scripture isn't really prayer if it doesn't turn into a conversation. That is why we read, think about what we have read, and then talk to God about what we are thinking. The fourth step is to listen, so it won't be a one-sided conversation. Many people find the *contemplatio* to be a difficult step; they worry about if they are "doing it right" or "if it's really God." Don't try so hard. Just be quiet and receive for a little while. Prayer is not so much about getting something from God as it is just being with God. We are using Scripture as a conversation starter, but conversations with God go deeper than words. Don't worry, I'll walk you through it.

Grace of the Week: Each week has a particular theme or focus. The first week will focus on the creation of the world, the plants, the animals, and human beings. The simplest things can be the easiest to forget, and the most profound when they are rediscovered. Pray for the grace to wonder anew at the marvel, mystery, and miracle of God's creation.

December 1 — Sunday
First Sunday of Advent

Preparation: Take a deep breath or two. Name three to five things you are grateful for. Say a prayer of thanksgiving to God for his blessings in your life.

Lectio: Today we begin our Advent journey. Let's take a moment to plan the trip. Take a look at the calendar and make some notes about how you can really enjoy Advent and Christmas this year.

You have twenty-five days until Christmas. But Christmas is not the only stop on our journey. We will stop to enjoy St. Nicholas Day this Friday. The Immaculate Conception, which is usually a holy day of obligation, gets transferred to Monday, December 9 this year. When will you put up your Christmas tree? Try to make it a family event. Whenever you put up your Christmas tree, I encourage you not to light it until after Christmas Mass. When will you put out your Christmas crèche? Take some time to plan these activities in advance.

For now, the only thing that you need to do is put out the Advent wreath and light the first candle. Everything else can happen in time. While you're looking at your calendar, you might want to plan a little time for baking, sending cards, present-wrapping, and quality family time — whatever makes Christmas special for you.

You might be feeling just a little anxious now that I brought all that up. It's normal to be anxious during Advent and Christmas. But this year we're not just going to plan Advent, we are also going to pray with Advent. What are God's plans for your Advent season? Read the Scripture passage slowly and prayerfully.

LUKE 21:25–28, 34–36 (LECTIONARY)

Jesus said to his disciples: "There will be signs in the sun, the moon, and the stars, and on earth nations will be in dismay, perplexed by the roaring of the sea and the waves. People will die of fright in anticipation of what is coming upon the world, for the powers of the heavens will be shaken. And then they will see the Son of Man coming in a cloud with power and great glory. But when these signs begin to happen, stand erect and raise your heads because your redemption is at hand.

"Beware that your hearts do not become drowsy from carousing and drunkenness and the anxieties of daily life, and that day catch you by surprise like a trap. For that day will assault everyone who lives on the face of the earth. Be vigilant at all times and pray that you have the strength to escape the tribulations that are imminent and to stand before the Son of Man."

Meditatio: What do you most remember from Christmas last year? Was it the gifts, the decorations, the baked goods, the parties, the cards — all the things that you stress about? Or was it something else? Let your mind drift back to last year and perhaps journal whatever you remember.

The coming of Jesus should excite us. We should stand erect and raise our heads knowing that our Lord and Savior is on his way to meet us. We must be vigilant to meet the Lord; the word in Latin is *vigilate*. The vigils were the night watches; soldiers would stay up and watch to protect the camp from attacks that might happen under cover of darkness. But watching for the Lord means not so much sleepless nights, but a watchful heart. A prayerful heart is a watchful heart. So, to do Advent well, we need to be prepared to pray well.

I have found that these two ingredients help me to pray well: time and place.

When will you pray? I like to pray right when I get up in the morning. Some people like to pray in the quiet of the evening. It may not happen exactly as you planned every day, but if you don't plan it, chances are it won't happen. Plan a time for prayer.

Where will you pray? If you don't already have a prayer room or a prayer corner, make one. It should be free of distractions and full of things that help you focus on God. I find that having a special place just for prayer is a really important ingredient in a successful prayer routine. Plan a place for prayer.

Now go back and read the Scripture passage a second time.

***Oratio*:** Let's not just plan for a good Advent, let's also pray about it. You "stand before the Son of Man" every time you pray. Ask God for the strength to pray well this Advent season. Ask God to show you his plans for your Christmas and help you accomplish them. Ask God to help you focus on the things that really matter and to let go of the things that don't matter.

And it starts with a simple question: What do you really want for Christmas this year?

***Contemplatio*:** Read the passage a third time. Now just try to receive whatever it is that God wants to give you. Don't try too hard to receive. Just be open to whatever feeling, image, thought, or idea might rise to the surface. Feelings of peace, comfort, or clarity often accompany the presence of God. The point of this last step is not so much to get something from God but more to just be with the God who loves you and will be with you through Advent and Christmas. Just be with the Lord for a couple of minutes before looking at the questions below.

SUGGESTIONS FOR JOURNALING

After each prayer time I will offer a few questions. This is not a test or quiz. The questions are provided to help you sift your prayer time. You may have already had a wonderful prayer time and have no need of these questions. Other times you might find that nothing seems to have "happened" in your prayer time, and the questions might tease out something of the gift or blessing you received. Use whatever you find helpful and skip the rest. It's your journey.

1. My favorite thing about last year's Christmas was ...
2. Last Christmas I struggled the most with ...
3. I get the most joy from ...
4. What are the things that matter most, that need to be a priority in my time budget this Christmas? What are the things that actually don't matter all that much, which I can let go of this year?
5. Where and when will I pray?
6. What is God's desire for my Christmas journey?
7. What do I really want for Christmas this year?

Now, just be still for a moment; the Lord is here with you.

The most important part of our Advent journey is an attitude of thanksgiving. So, thank God for today's prayer time and close with an Our Father.

December 2 — Monday
Monday of the First Week of Advent

Preparation: *Come, Holy Spirit, enlighten the eyes of my heart* (see Eph 1:18).

Lectio: Our pilgrimage begins with the creation story, but perhaps not the version that you might have been expecting. The Bible tells the story of creation twice. The first story shows how creation unfolds in an orderly way over the course of six days, starting with light and ending with the creation of man and woman (see Gn 1:1–2:3). The second story tells it from the opposite perspective, beginning with the creation of man. Read through the passage slowly and prayerfully, and try to see it with fresh eyes.

GENESIS 2:4–7

This is the story of the heavens and the earth at their creation. When the LORD God made the earth and the heavens — there was no field shrub on earth and no grass of the field had sprouted, for the LORD God had sent no rain upon the earth and there was no man to till the ground, but a stream was welling up out of the earth and watering all the surface of the ground — then the LORD God formed the man out of the dust of the ground and blew into his nostrils the breath of life, and the man became a living being.

Meditatio: The ancients understood that when a human being dies, he turns into dust. So, our ancient authors pictured God starting from dust and ending with a well-formed human being, like a potter molding clay. There is a play here on words between the Hebrew *adam* (man) and *adama* (ground). Picture the care with which God shapes the bones, muscles, eyes, teeth, and hair. Then God bends down and shares some of his own life with this being. The Hebrew word for "breath" (*ruach*) also means "spirit" and "wind." It is as though the creature lives because God has shared some of his own life with it. What would it feel like to be created? Think about what it means to be shaped by God, to bear his fingerprints on your body and his warm breath in your lungs. Then read the passage again.

Oratio: The first thing that Adam would see when he woke up was the God who had just created him, perhaps beaming proudly at his new creation, like an artist admiring his masterpiece. Look at God and let him look at you. What words come to your mind? Speak to your Creator. Ask him about yourself or about him, or just thank him for creating you. Take some deep breaths. Then read the passage one more time.

Contemplatio: Open your heart to receive whatever God might want to give you. Don't sweat this step. Think of it like sensing the direction of the wind or basking for a moment in the sun's light. Contemplation is about being, but being in relationship. Just be with the God who has created you and is proud of the work that he has done. Receive his love for you in whatever way you can.

SUGGESTIONS FOR JOURNALING

1. What was my most noticeable thought, feeling, or desire during prayer time today?
2. What was on my heart? What did I bring to God?
3. Did I notice God's presence or his response to me in any particular way? If I did, how would I describe that? If not, how did I feel about that?
4. Does it feel different to look at my own hands and realize that they were shaped by God, and that no one else has my fingerprints?
5. One day I will take my final breath. What does each breath mean to me? How do my breaths connect me with God? What do my breaths mean to God?

_____

_____

_____

_____

_____

_____

_____

_____

_____

_____

_____

_____

_____

_____

_____

_____

_____

_____

Spend a few minutes in wonder and awe at the mystery and marvel of creation that is you! Let gratitude rise in your heart. Then close with an Our Father.

December 3 — Tuesday
Tuesday of the First Week of Advent

ST. FRANCIS XAVIER

A native of Spain, Francis Xavier met St. Ignatius of Loyola while studying at the University of Paris. He became one of the first seven members of the Society of Jesus (the Jesuits). He was sent to preach the Gospel in the Orient. In ten years of missionary work, he brought more than thirty thousand souls to the light of Christ. His travels took him to India and Japan, and he died on the doorstep of China. He is a patron saint of missions. He reminds us that the Gospel is meant for all people, and that every child is a child of God.

Preparation: *Come, Holy Spirit, enlighten the eyes of my heart.* Briefly review yesterday's prayer time (or the last time you prayed with *Oriens*, if you missed yesterday). Spend a minute being grateful for how God has been with you in your prayer time and indeed in all the moments of this week.

Lectio: In your own words ask God to help you wonder anew at the marvel, mystery, and miracle of his creation. The creation around us belongs to God. He has given it to us as a sacred trust. We exercise lordship over all creatures, but we ourselves are servants of the Lord. Read the passage slowly and prayerfully.

GENESIS 2:8–9, 15–17

The LORD God planted a garden in Eden, in the east, and placed there the man whom he had formed. Out of the ground the LORD God made grow every tree that was delightful to look at and good for food, with the tree of life in the middle of the garden and the tree of the knowledge of good and evil.

The LORD God then took the man and settled him in the garden of Eden, to cultivate and care for it. The LORD

God gave the man this order: You are free to eat from any of the trees of the garden except the tree of knowledge of good and evil. From that tree you shall not eat; when you eat from it you shall die.

Meditatio: The creation that surrounds man was made for him to feed him and delight him. Some theologians interpret the various trees as symbolizing all the pleasures and delights of life; he lives in a veritable "garden of delight" (one possible meaning for the word *Eden*). The world was made for him, but it does not belong to him; both he and his home belong to the God who made them. This God entrusts man with a specific job, "to cultivate and care for it." Picture the kind of fancy, cultivated gardens that often surround European mansions. God is the master and man is the gardener or caretaker. He can use everything except for one single tree that is off-limits. What thoughts or feelings arise in your heart? Read the passage again prayerfully.

Oratio: When have you experienced being a steward of God's creation? What has God entrusted to you — life, land, children to care for, gifts of talents? Have you used them in ways that made the master proud of you? Have you respected the rules that he has set for his garden? God is here with you and ready to listen. Speak to him from your heart. Then read the passage one more time.

Contemplatio: Open your heart and let your master speak to you. Receive whatever it is that God wants to give you. You are his steward, his caretaker, his friend. Rest quietly for a minute or two and marvel at all that has been entrusted to you.

SUGGESTIONS FOR JOURNALING
1. What most delights me about the creation that surrounds me?
2. How do I see myself as a steward of creation? What has been entrusted to me?
3. How has God set rules or limits for me? What things are "off-limits" to me because I am the steward and not the master?
4. I feel most humbled by …

5. I felt God saying to me …
6. I left prayer wanting …
7. One change that I can make, that will help remind me that I am a steward and not the master, is …

After you've journaled, spend a minute in gratitude for the prayer time you've just had. Close with an Our Father.

December 4 — Wednesday
Wednesday of the First Week of Advent

Preparation: *Come, Holy Spirit, enlighten the eyes of my heart.* Flip back to yesterday's prayer and recall a blessing that you experienced. Spend a minute savoring God's loving care for all his creatures and especially his care for you.

Lectio: In your own words ask God to help you wonder anew at the marvel, mystery, and miracle of his creation. Read today's passage slowly and prayerfully.

GENESIS 2:18–25

The LORD God said: It is not good for the man to be alone. I will make a helper suited to him. So the LORD God formed out of the ground all the wild animals and all the birds of the air, and he brought them to the man to see what he would call them; whatever the man called each living creature was then its name. The man gave names to all the tame animals, all the birds of the air, and all the wild animals; but none proved to be a helper suited to the man.

So the LORD God cast a deep sleep on the man, and while he was asleep, he took out one of his ribs and closed up its place with flesh. The LORD God then built the rib that he had taken from the man into a woman. When he brought her to the man, the man said:

"This one, at last, is bone of my bones
and flesh of my flesh;
This one shall be called 'woman,'
for out of man this one has been taken."

That is why a man leaves his father and mother and clings

to his wife, and the two of them become one body.
    The man and his wife were both naked, yet they felt no shame.

Meditatio: God makes all kinds of living beings, and the man helps by naming each one (in the Bible, naming something is a sign of authority over it). Despite all the delights that surround him, something is missing that the man can't quite name. Only when he wakes up to the woman of his dreams does he realize his desire to have a relationship with someone who can receive his love and love him in return. Man was made by love and for love. The two are perfectly comfortable together. Read the passage again slowly.

Oratio: What is this prayer time stirring up inside of you? Is something missing in your life that you can't quite name? Notice the feelings that are stirring inside of you, then speak to God honestly about them. You can be perfectly comfortable with God. Share your heart with the one who made it. When you are done talking, read the passage one more time, or just the word or phrase that really spoke to you.

Contemplatio: Open your heart to conversation with God. The one who made you knows your deepest desires. He also knows his plans to fulfill them. What is it that God wants to give you, or might be saying back to you? Don't try too hard to "get it." Just be open to receive.

SUGGESTIONS FOR JOURNALING

1. Which of the animals that God has created most delights me?
2. How have I cooperated with God's work of creation, working alongside God in my own little way?
3. Was there a time in my life when I experienced a longing that I didn't understand or couldn't really name?
4. My life seemed to click when …
5. I ended prayer wanting …
6. If I could put God's desire for me into words, I would say that he wants …

After you've journaled, close with a brief conversation giving thanks to God for your prayer experience. Then pray an Our Father.

December 5 — Thursday
Thursday of the First Week of Advent

Preparation: *Come, Holy Spirit, enlighten the eyes of my heart.* Flip back to yesterday's prayer and recall a blessing that you experienced. Spend a minute savoring God's loving care for all his creatures and especially his care for you.

Lectio: In your own words ask God to help you wonder anew at the marvel, mystery, and miracle of human and divine love. Some people are scandalized to discover a love poem right in the middle of the Bible. They don't seem to realize that the Bible begins with a wedding (see Gn 2:18–25) and ends with a wedding (Rv 19:1–9). Do you think that God might be trying to tell us something? Read today's passage slowly and prayerfully.

SONG OF SONGS 2:8–14

> The sound of my lover! here he comes
> springing across the mountains,
> leaping across the hills.
> My lover is like a gazelle
> or a young stag.
> See! He is standing behind our wall,
> gazing through the windows,
> peering through the lattices.
> My lover speaks and says to me,
> "Arise, my friend, my beautiful one,
> and come!
> For see, the winter is past,
> the rains are over and gone.
> The flowers appear on the earth,
> the time of pruning the vines has come,
> and the song of the turtledove is heard in our land.

> The fig tree puts forth its figs,
>   and the vines, in bloom, give forth fragrance.
> Arise, my friend, my beautiful one,
>   and come!
> My dove in the clefts of the rock,
>   in the secret recesses of the cliff,
> Let me see your face,
>   let me hear your voice,
> For your voice is sweet,
>   and your face is lovely."

Meditatio: More than anything, two people who love each other long to be together. This poem is full of the longing between young lovers. When was the first time that you fell in love? What did it feel like? How did it change you? We sometimes chuckle when our siblings, friends, or children fall deeply in love. They act like they are the first people in the world to ever be in love, and no one has ever experienced something so amazing as this! And yet, when we reflect on our own experiences, we realize that falling in love always catches us off guard and sweeps us along. Even when you fall in love again with a spouse after twenty or thirty years of marriage, it is like tasting an old wine that surprises us with how good it has gotten. There is something about true love that is always fresh and new. Notice what word or phrase really speaks to you as you read this passage a second time.

Oratio: What thoughts, feelings, or desires are rising in your heart? They may also be fears, failures, or disappointments. Love is the most beautiful, powerful, and poignant experience. And that also means that it can be the most difficult, devastating, and heartbreaking experience. But you have never experienced it alone. Because God is love, every experience of real love is an experience of God. Turn to the God who loves you. Share with him what is on your heart. Be completely honest with him. When you have poured out your heart, read the passage a third time slowly and prayerfully.

Contemplatio: God knows the depths of your heart just like he knew the desires in Adam's heart. Now receive what God wants to share with you. Is there some new insight or understanding that emerges? How does your experience look different in the light of God's love? Rest in his love for you for a few minutes before moving on.

SUGGESTIONS FOR JOURNALING

1. Falling in love is like …
2. I am afraid that …
3. God wanted me to know …
4. The deepest desire that I have right now is for …
5. I feel most satisfied, joyful, and peaceful when …
6. I ended prayer wanting …

_____

_____

_____

_____

_____

_____

_____

_____

_____

_____

_____

_____

_____

_____

_____

_____

_____

_____

_____

_____

_____

_____

After you've journaled, close with a conversation with God giving thanks for your prayer experience. Then pray an Our Father.

December 6 — Friday
Friday of the First Week of Advent

SAINT NICHOLAS, BISHOP

Saint Nicholas was the bishop of Myra in modern-day Turkey. He died on this day around AD 350. He is one of the most popular Christian saints, though very little is known about him. He is a patron of mariners, merchants, bakers, travelers, and children. There are many legends associated with him, one of which is that he brings little gifts to children on his feast day. He is known for his generosity. Ask him to help you experience more deeply the generosity of God that led him to create human beings.

Preparation: *Come, Holy Spirit, enlighten the eyes of my heart.* Briefly review yesterday's prayer time (or the last time you prayed with *Oriens*, if you missed yesterday). Spend a minute being grateful for how God has been with you in your prayer time and indeed in all the moments of this week.

Lectio: In your own words ask God to help you wonder anew at the marvel, mystery, and miracle of his creation. The creation around us belongs to God. He has given it to us as a sacred trust. We exercise lordship over all creatures, but we ourselves are servants of the Lord. Read the passage slowly and prayerfully.

PSALM 8:2–10

O Lord, our Lord,
 how awesome is your name through all the earth!
I will sing of your majesty above the heavens
 with the mouths of babes and infants.
You have established a bulwark against your foes,
 to silence enemy and avenger.
When I see your heavens, the work of your fingers,

the moon and stars that you set in place —
What is man that you are mindful of him,
and a son of man that you care for him?
Yet you have made him little less than a god,
crowned him with glory and honor.
You have given him rule over the works of your hands,
put all things at his feet:
All sheep and oxen,
even the beasts of the field,
The birds of the air, the fish of the sea,
and whatever swims the paths of the seas.
O Lord, our Lord,
how awesome is your name through all the earth!

Meditatio: There is only one God; how then can human beings be "little less than a god"? We have been made in the image and likeness of God. How has God crowned you with glory and honor? Have you used dominion over all creatures? Was God right to entrust you with his creation or have you proved less than trustworthy? Read the passage again slowly. Notice whatever word or phrase jumps out at you.

Oratio: God has not simply abandoned us or any other part of creation. Though we may not notice his quiet presence, he is always with us. The "babes and infants" do not recognize political correctness and tend to speak truth as they see it. God wants the same from us, his children. Speak to the Lord with childlike honesty. The Lord will listen patiently, so have no fear of not saying quite the right thing. Speak to him from your heart. When you are done, read the passage a third time.

Contemplatio: This time just be open to receive. Picture the heavens, the moon, and the stars, steady reminders of God's awesome power. How might God respond to what you have shared with him? Maybe it is a thought, word, or feeling. Just spend a few minutes letting God look at you with love, with you gazing back at him. Enjoy the presence of God before you move on.

SUGGESTIONS FOR JOURNALING

1. If I were to use my own words, I would say that "crowned with glory and honor" means …
2. I most marvel at creation when …
3. I am most humbled by …
4. I am most grateful for …
5. I have experienced God's care when …
6. I feel called to …

_____

_____

_____

_____

_____

_____

_____

_____

_____

_____

_____

_____

_____

_____

_____

After you've journaled, close with a brief conversation giving thanks to God for your prayer experience. You may be tempted to skip this as you've already talked to God. But keep in mind that the goal of prayer is not to have nice notes in a journal, but to have a deeper encounter with the God who loves you. So, after praying, reflecting, and journaling, have one more little chat with God. Think of it like talking to a friend as you walk them out to their car after a nice visit. You thank them for their visit and their friendship, don't you? Spend a moment saying, "Thank you, God." Then pray an Our Father.

December 7 — Saturday
Saturday of the First Week of Advent

REVIEW

Preparation: *Come, Holy Spirit, enlighten the eyes of my heart.* Instead of spending time with a new passage, we will pray with the passages that most spoke to you in this past week. Saint Ignatius called this kind of prayer time a "repetition." The idea behind a repetition is not so much to do a prayer passage all over again, but to go back to the place that you most noticed God's presence and felt loved by God. You return to that place in order to deepen the encounter and the conversation with God. Flip back through your past week's journal entries. Notice what emerged in the conversations. Here are some questions to help you:

1. The prayer time that I enjoyed most and got the most out of was …

2. The prayer time that I really struggled with was … What made it hard for me?

3. Where did I notice the presence of God? What did his presence feel like, or how did it affect me?

4. What was God doing, saying, or giving me this week?

5. How did I respond to what God was doing?

6. I'm most grateful for …

7. Is there one clear image of God's loving presence that emerged from my prayer during this first week? Or was there a word, phrase, or message that really touched me?

_____

_____

_____

_____

_____

_____

_____

_____

_____

_____

_____

_____

_____

_____

_____

_____

_____

_____

Savor that image of God's loving presence. Rest there for a few minutes. Then thank God for today's prayer time and end with an Our Father.

Week Two

Week Two

Imaginative Prayer

Did you enjoy *lectio divina*? If you struggled with a prayer routine last week, don't let that bother you. Don't go back and try to pray all the hours that you missed. Just pick up today and pray this day well. Remember that good prayer is not about having lots of great notes in your book. Good prayer is about spending quality time with the God who loves you. If you spent any quality time with God last week, you did well.

This week we will learn a new prayer form called Imaginative Prayer. St. Ignatius of Loyola seems to have invented this prayer form while he was recuperating from battle wounds at his family's castle. He wanted to pass the time reading courtly romance novels, but none could be found. All they had was a book on the lives of the saints and a book that retold the Gospels (like the Christian miniseries *The Chosen*). He began to read these books and imagine himself meeting Jesus in Bible times or living the life of a great saint. Other times he would think back to his favorite romance novels and imagine himself fighting great battles and winning the hand of a princess. His courtly daydreams left him feeling empty. However, his saintly daydreams gave him a sense of peace and joy that lasted. One day he noticed the difference and marveled at it. This simple insight was the beginning of his conversion.

Many people are skeptical of imaginative prayer. They wonder if they are inventing things and if God is really speaking to them through their prayer. Your imagination was created by God as a faculty of the intellect. It is a powerful tool and can be used to make Scripture come alive. God is with you right now as you read these words. But you are more aware of your location in space and time, how you spent Saturday night, and what is coming up today. Through the imagination we are able to step out of the here-and-now temporarily so as to access the deeper spiritual presence of God with us. The imagination becomes a springboard for an encounter with God.

Remember that prayer is really about spending time with the God who loves us. It's not about filling pages of a journal with amazing insights or experiences. If you are open to an encounter, then God will come and meet you. The imagination is only a conversation starter.

Grace of the Week: We are surrounded by God's creation. We are also creatures who were made by God for a relationship with him. This week we will explore our fall from a relationship with God and into the deep darkness of sin and death. Pray for the grace to experience how much pain this separation causes God, so as to experience a greater longing for relationship with him.

December 8 — Sunday
Second Sunday of Advent

Preparation: *Come, Holy Spirit, enlighten the eyes of my heart.* Turn back to yesterday and look at that image of God's loving care for you that emerged in your review time. Use your imagination to picture that moment again. Spend about a minute just resting in that experience and savoring the unconditional love with which God loves you.

Set the Scene: Ask God in your own words for the grace to experience how much pain our sinful separation causes God, so as to experience a deeper longing for relationship with him. Read the passage below. As you do, set the scene in your mind. Picture John the Baptist wearing the rough cloak of a prophet and wandering through the region of the Jordan calling the people to repentance.

LUKE 3:1–6 (LECTIONARY)

In the fifteenth year of the reign of Tiberius Caesar, when Pontius Pilate was governor of Judea, and Herod was tetrarch of Galilee, and his brother Philip tetrarch of the region of Ituraea and Trachonitis, and Lysanias was tetrarch of Abilene, during the high priesthood of Annas and Caiaphas, the word of God came to John the son of Zechariah in the desert. John went throughout the whole region of the Jordan, proclaiming a baptism of repentance for the forgiveness of sins, as it is written in the book of the words of the prophet Isaiah:

> *A voice of one crying out in the desert:*
> *"Prepare the way of the Lord,*
>   *make straight his paths.*
> *Every valley shall be filled*
>   *and every mountain and hill shall be made low.*
> *The winding roads shall be made straight,*
>   *and the rough ways made smooth,*
> *and all flesh shall see the salvation of God."*

Action: Saint Luke wants to make sure his readers understand that the coming of Jesus really happened, in a real time and a real place. He names the major and minor players in politics and religion. Then his focus shifts to the wilderness where we see and hear the last in a long line of prophetic voices. Seven hundred years earlier, the Prophet Isaiah started to prepare the way for this prophet who will prepare the way for Jesus Christ. The Jordan River begins at the Sea of Galilee and flows down to the Dead Sea, the lowest place on Earth. This setting is itself a parable. He is warning his hearers that just "going with the flow" of modern life will lead you to a dead end, a place of spiritual death. How do the people receive this message? Picture the people who begin to "swim against the current" and those who keep "going with the flow."

Acknowledge: As you process this scene, notice what is happening in you. What thought or feeling resonates with you? What part of the passage is speaking to you? Read the passage a second time.

Relate: Turn to God and share with him what is on your heart. This can be a more challenging part of the prayer. Think of it this way: You are watching John the Baptist wandering from place to place, preaching repentance, and inviting people to new life. You watch the people listening and pondering, accepting or dismissing the call. As you watch, you realize that God is with you, and he too is watching the scene. After watching for a while, turn and look at God. Let him look at you. Talk to him about what you noticed, thought, or felt.

Receive: What was in God's heart when his Spirit was speaking through John the Baptist? What is in God's heart for you? Receive whatever it is that God wants to give you — his thoughts, feelings, and desires. Read the passage a third time, or perhaps just the part that you feel most drawn to. As you do, focus on God and let him speak to you, or just quietly receive what he wants to give you.

Respond: Now answer him again. Respond to what you have received. Just be with the Lord and savor his loving presence for a minute or two before moving on.

SUGGESTIONS FOR JOURNALING

1. While imagining the scene, what stood out to me was ...
2. I feel moved to repent of ...
3. When God entered the scene, I felt ...
4. I sensed God calling me to ...
5. God wants me to experience new life in what area of my life?
6. I ended prayer with a sense that ...

After you've journaled, close with a brief conversation giving thanks to God for your prayer experience. Then pray an Our Father.

December 9 — Monday
Solemnity of the Immaculate Conception

The Christian Church has long believed that the Blessed Virgin Mary was preserved free from all sin starting at the very moment of her conception. Christians have celebrated this feast for more than 1,200 years, but it was officially declared a dogma by Bl. Pope Pius IX in 1854. Four years later, Our Lady appeared to Saint Bernadette at Lourdes, France, and told her, "I am the Immaculate Conception." Today's feast is usually a holy day of obligation for Catholics, except when December 8 is a Sunday and the feast is bumped to Monday, December 9 (or when the feast falls on a Monday). Then it becomes what I like to call a "holy day of opportunity." You have the opportunity to celebrate the day that Our Lady was conceived without sin in her mother's womb, and receive blessings to yourself become more free from original sin.

Preparation: *Come, Holy Spirit, enlighten the eyes of my heart.* Call to mind your recent experience of God's loving care. Spend about a minute just resting in that experience and savoring the unconditional love of the Father for his child. Let gratitude rise in your heart.

Set the Scene: Ask God in your own words for the grace to experience how much pain our sinful separation causes God, so as to experience a deeper longing for relationship with him. The Bible tells us that God would come walking in the garden at the breezy time of day (shortly before sunset in the geography of the Holy Land). He is surveying his property and visiting his favorite creatures. But all is not well today. Instead of coming to meet him, Adam and Eve hide themselves among the trees of the garden. Picture the scene in your mind as you read through this passage.

GENESIS 3:9–15, 20 (LECTIONARY)
After the man, Adam, had eaten of the tree, the Lord

God called to the man and asked him, "Where are you?"
He answered, "I heard you in the garden; but I was afraid,
because I was naked, so I hid myself." Then he asked,
"Who told you that you were naked? You have eaten,
then, from the tree of which I had forbidden you to eat!"
The man replied, "The woman whom you put here with
me — she gave me fruit from the tree, and so I ate it." The
LORD God then asked the woman, "Why did you do such
a thing?" The woman answered, "The serpent tricked me
into it, so I ate it."

Then the LORD God said to the serpent: "Because you
have done this, you shall be banned from all the animals
and from all the wild creatures; on your belly shall you
crawl, and dirt shall you eat all the days of your life. I will
put enmity between you and the woman, and between
your offspring and hers; he will strike at your head, while
you strike at his heel."

The man called his wife Eve, because she became the
mother of all the living.

Action: I always pictured them hiding in the bushes, but Genesis 3:8 says, "When they heard the sound of the LORD God walking about in the garden at the breezy time of the day, the man and his wife hid themselves from the LORD God among the trees of the garden." Since the trees symbolize the delights and pleasures of the created world, they are using worldly pleasures to hide from God. Does this sound familiar? But also, trees don't cover us very well. Adam and Eve think that they are hidden, but God has no problem spotting them. Notice each of the main actors in this drama. What motivates their actions?

Acknowledge: How does it feel for Adam to be caught red-handed, naked and afraid of God? When have you felt guilty, ashamed, naked? Are there feelings, or perhaps the memory of an experience, that reading this passage stirs up inside of you? Or if nothing personal comes to mind, imagine how Adam and Eve would have felt. Shame has the effect of driving us away and causing us to hide. Notice your strongest thought, feeling, or desire. Read the passage again.

Relate: God is with you right here and right now. There is no need to be afraid of him or hide from him. Turn your heart to God. Speak to him in your heart. Share with him what this passage stirred up within you. Sometimes the biggest feeling might be that we don't want to share our feelings with God. Can you tell God that?

Receive: We learned yesterday of God's desire to bring the captives home. God would love to forgive Adam and Eve but they turn away from him instead of toward him. How does God feel as the man and the woman hide from him? This time receive whatever is in God's heart for you: his thought, feeling, desire. If you find yourself struggling, know that you don't have to try so hard. Just be open to receive. Many times, God gives something simple like a feeling of peace, a sense of his presence, or a sense that he understands what we are going through. Read the passage a third time.

Respond: Receive what God has to give you, then answer him again. It may be just a simple "Thank you." Or it may stir up more to talk about. Perhaps you enter into a little conversation. Enjoy the presence of God for a minute or two before moving on.

SUGGESTIONS FOR JOURNALING
1. When I read this passage, what jumped out at me was …
2. My strongest thought, feeling, or desire was …
3. What part of my life, my actions and decisions, is shaped by shame?
4. I saw with new eyes …
5. I ended prayer wanting …
6. The desire of God's heart is …

_____

_____

_____

_____

_____

_____

_____

_____

_____

_____

_____

_____

_____

_____

_____

_____

After you've journaled, close with a brief conversation giving thanks to God for your prayer experience. Then pray an Our Father.

December 10 — Tuesday
Tuesday of the Second Week of Advent

Preparation: *Come, Holy Spirit, enlighten the eyes of my heart.* Call to mind an image of God's loving care for you that has emerged in your prayer. Spend about a minute just resting in that experience and savoring the unconditional love with which God loves you. Let gratitude rise in your heart.

Set the Scene: Ask God in your own words for the grace to experience how much pain our sinful separation causes God, so as to experience a deeper longing for relationship with him. The story continues from yesterday. Adam and Eve stand before God wearing loin cloths of fig leaves that they had sewed together. Like a just judge, God is passing sentence on them.

GENESIS 3:16–19
To the woman he said:

> I will intensify your toil in childbearing;
>> in pain you shall bring forth children.
> Yet your urge shall be for your husband,
>> and he shall rule over you.

To the man he said: Because you listened to your wife and ate from the tree about which I commanded you, You shall not eat from it,

> Cursed is the ground because of you!
>> In toil you shall eat its yield
>> all the days of your life.
> Thorns and thistles it shall bear for you,
>> and you shall eat the grass of the field.

> By the sweat of your brow
>   you shall eat bread,
> Until you return to the ground,
>   from which you were taken;
> For you are dust,
>   and to dust you shall return.

Action: Picture every generation of women panting in pain as they struggle to bring life into the world. Picture generations of men fighting with thorns and thistles and plows, sweating for the food that their families desperately need for survival. In the end, whether in childbirth or as a child or in old age, they all die. Their family digs a grave and recites, "For you are dust, and to dust you shall return" over an unbroken succession of graves and coffins and burial grounds. Read the passage a second time.

Acknowledge: Adam and Eve are sentenced to hard labor — for her, the labor of bearing children; for him, the labor of tilling the earth. Because of Adam and Eve, men and women continue to toil and labor. Raising children, buying Christmas gifts, figuring out a way to pay for them all … feel the heaviness of the sentence that will rest on all human beings for all future generations. And lest we claim innocence, we have all sinned and fallen short of the glory of God, and we have each added to the burden of sin that weighs down humanity. When do you feel this burden weighing heavily upon you? What is your strongest thought, feeling, or desire?

Relate: God is with you right here and right now. Turn your heart to God. Speak to him in your heart. Share with him the burdens that you carry.

Receive: Remember that God is more than a judge. He is a Father deeply grieved by his children's sinfulness. He starts to unfold a plan to remedy their sinfulness. Christians have long believed that Jesus's death forgave even Adam and Eve, and that God took them to heaven in the end. Read the passage a third time. This time receive whatever is in God's heart for you: his thoughts, feelings, or desires. He loves you and is with you in the midst of your burdens. He desires to remedy sin and to help you carry this burden. Just be open to receive, without fear or expectation.

Respond: Receive what God wants to give you, then answer him back. It may be just a simple "Thank you." It may be a feeling of peace or a realization that you are not alone. Converse with the Lord for a minute or two and then spend a few minutes savoring his merciful love.

SUGGESTIONS FOR JOURNALING

1. My strongest thought, feeling, or desire was …
2. I feel the burden of original sin when …
3. I see the love of God in a new way …
4. I sensed God communicating to me …
5. A new insight or understanding I received was …
6. God wants to give me …

After you've journaled, close with a brief conversation giving thanks to God for your prayer experience. Then pray an Our Father.

December 11 — Wednesday
Wednesday of the Second Week of Advent

Preparation: *Come, Holy Spirit, enlighten the eyes of my heart.* Call to mind a recent experience of God's loving care. Spend about a minute just resting in that experience and savoring the unconditional love with which God loves you. Let gratitude rise in your heart.

Set the Scene: Ask God in your own words for the grace to experience how much pain our sinful separation causes God, so as to experience a deeper longing for relationship with him. The Israelites are part of God's great project to rescue humanity from sin and death. They are meant to be a holy people, an example to the nations of what it looks like when we listen to God and follow his commandments. But instead, they have sunk into wickedness. Read the passage to set the scene.

ISAIAH 1:2–4, 15–20

Hear, O heavens, and listen, O earth,
for the LORD speaks:
Sons have I raised and reared,
but they have rebelled against me!
An ox knows its owner,
and an ass, its master's manger;
But Israel does not know,
my people has not understood.
Ah! Sinful nation, people laden with wickedness,
evil offspring, corrupt children!
They have forsaken the LORD,
spurned the Holy One of Israel,
apostatized.
When you spread out your hands,
I will close my eyes to you;
Though you pray the more,

I will not listen.
Your hands are full of blood!
   Wash yourselves clean!
Put away your misdeeds from before my eyes;
   cease doing evil;
   learn to do good.
Make justice your aim: redress the wronged,
   hear the orphan's plea, defend the widow.
Come now, let us set things right,
   says the LORD*:*
Though your sins be like scarlet,
   they may become white as snow;
Though they be red like crimson,
   they may become white as wool.
If you are willing, and obey,
   you shall eat the good things of the land;
But if you refuse and resist,
   you shall be eaten by the sword:
   for the mouth of the LORD *has spoken!*

Action: You may find it hard to imagine this scene. It might help to call to mind recent news stories of bloodshed, mass shootings, and war. Every day there are thefts, frauds, sexual assaults, and murders perpetrated by people who are baptized into the family of God. Even clergy are guilty of monstrous crimes. These are the kinds of scenes that God is seeing as he speaks through the Prophet Isaiah. Read the passage again.

Acknowledge: Notice what it stirs up inside of you: thoughts, feelings, desires. Remember that God is a loving Father. It hurts him to see his children punished, but it hurts him more to see them doing evil. God wants his children to live good lives. If they refuse to turn from wickedness, he will be forced to punish them severely. It is right to be angry at the injustice around us. But are we not also guilty of tearing down our brothers and sisters, exploiting them or damaging their good name? The first victim of evil is always God himself.

Relate: Turn your heart to God and speak to him. Share with God what this passage stirred up within you. Now let him look at you with love. How does he respond?

Receive: Read the passage a third time. This time receive whatever is in God's heart for you — his thoughts, feelings, desires. How does it make God suffer when he sees his children hurting one another? What does he want for his children? Don't think too hard about this step. Just notice what comes up in the prayer.

Respond: Receive what God has to give you. Then respond in some way. Perhaps you need to say, "I'm sorry." Perhaps God is inviting you to some kind of action. Be with the Lord for a minute or two before moving on.

SUGGESTIONS FOR JOURNALING

1. I feel the weight of human sin when …
2. A new insight or understanding that I received was …
3. I felt convicted that …
4. I sensed God communicating to me …
5. I see sin in a new and different light …
6. I feel the Spirit of God moving me to a new way of acting, responding, or thinking …

After you've journaled, close with a brief conversation giving thanks to God for your prayer experience. Then pray an Our Father.

December 12 — Thursday
Thursday of the Second Week of Advent

FEAST OF OUR LADY OF GUADALUPE

On December 12, 1532, a native of Mexico called Juan Diego arrived at the bishop's palace clutching something in his tilma (a blanket with a hole for the head, like a poncho, woven of agave fiber). He refused to show it to anyone but the bishop. The bishop's servants made him wait for a long time before finally ushering him into the bishop's room. He unfolded his mantle, and Castilian roses tumbled out onto the floor. Even more surprisingly, a miraculous image of the Our Lady herself was imprinted on his tilma. A shrine was built in which to house the miraculous tilma, and next to it a little house for Juan Diego. He spent the rest of his life telling his story as millions of native Aztecs, Chichimecas, and other indigenous Central Americans converted to the Catholic Faith. The image hangs today in the shrine of Our Lady of Guadalupe on the outskirts of Mexico City. It testifies to Mary's love for all people, including you.

Preparation: *Come, Holy Spirit, enlighten the eyes of my heart.* Be present to the God who is always present to you. Call to mind how you have experienced his loving care for you and spend the first minute of your prayer just resting in the free, unearned gift of loving and being loved. Let gratitude rise in your heart.

Set the scene: Ask God in your own words for the grace to experience how much pain our sinful separation causes God, so as to experience a deeper longing for relationship with him. Today's Scripture passage is taken from the Book of Revelation. It is a dramatic and imaginative vision of the struggle between good and evil. Read the passage once to set the scene in your mind.

REVELATION 11:19A; 12:1–6A, 10AB (LECTIONARY)

God's temple in heaven was opened, and the ark of his

covenant could be seen in the temple.

A great sign appeared in the sky, a woman clothed with the sun, with the moon under her feet, and on her head a crown of twelve stars. She was with child and wailed aloud in pain as she labored to give birth. Then another sign appeared in the sky; it was a huge red dragon, with seven heads and ten horns, and on its heads were seven diadems. Its tail swept away a third of the stars in the sky and hurled them down to the earth. Then the dragon stood before the woman about to give birth, to devour her child when she gave birth. She gave birth to a son, a male child, destined to rule all the nations with an iron rod. Her child was caught up to God and his throne. The woman herself fled into the desert where she had a place prepared by God.

Then I heard a loud voice in heaven say: "Now have salvation and power come, and the Kingdom of our God and the authority of his Anointed."

Action: This passage is taken from today's feast day. The image left on Juan Diego's *tilma* shows a woman standing in front of the sun, with the moon under her feet, and wearing a blue-green cloak covered in stars. The sun and moon represented the most powerful Aztec gods. Our Lady is claiming to be more powerful than they are. Yet, she herself is not a god, as she is shown with head bowed and hands folded, reverently praying to God. She is pregnant with God's child.

Acknowledge: What do you think and feel as you picture the scene? What is the woman feeling? The woman and her child are not afraid to be humble and little, as God protects them and provides for them. They have the opposite attitude to Adam and Eve, who refused to accept being childlike. Does the thought of humbleness and littleness make you uncomfortable? Do you have a hard time trusting in God's care and protection? Read the passage a second time.

Relate: Where do you see God in today's Scripture passage? Turn to God and speak to him. Share your thoughts, feelings, and desires, the things that were stirred up by today's prayer time. If feelings of shame vulnerability or powerlessness arise, don't be afraid to share them with. Perhaps the woman clothed with the sun can help you voice what is in your heart.

Receive: Let God respond to what you have shared. Notice whatever thought, feeling, or desire God wants to communicate to you. Read the passage a third time.

Respond: Receive whatever new way God invites you to see this scene in Revelation, the woman, or your own life. Make room in your heart for God's way of seeing things. Then rest in God's love for you for a few minutes before moving on.

SUGGESTIONS FOR JOURNALING
1. I was surprised by …
2. I have a hard time believing that …
3. When I hear the words *humble* and *little*, I think of …
4. I have a newfound appreciation for …
5. I feel God calling me to a new way of seeing, thinking, or acting …

After you've journaled, close with a brief conversation giving thanks to God for your prayer experience. Then pray a Hail Mary.

December 13 — Friday
Friday of the Second Week of Advent

SAINT LUCY

Little is known about this young Christian girl from Syracuse in Sicily. It is said that a disappointed suitor denounced her as a Christian and she was executed in AD 304. She is one of just seven women mentioned by name in the Roman Canon (Eucharistic Prayer I) of the Mass. Her name comes from the Latin word *lux*, meaning light. Because of this, she is a patroness of eyesight. Her feast day is celebrated with the lighting of candles, particularly in Scandinavian countries. Pray that God will enlighten your eyes and help make you a light to others.

Preparation: *Come, Holy Spirit, enlighten the eyes of my heart.* Call to mind a recent experience of God's loving care. Spend about a minute just resting in that experience and savoring the unconditional love with which God loves you. Let gratitude rise in your heart.

Set the Scene: Ask God in your own words for the grace to experience how much pain our sinful separation causes God, so as to experience a deeper longing for relationship with him. Read the passage below. As you do, set the scene in your mind. Picture the looks on the faces of the captives as they were led away on foot by their enemies, wrapped in mourning and misery. Then picture them carried on royal thrones, wrapped in justice and glory.

BARUCH 5:1–9 (LECTIONARY)

Jerusalem, take off your robe of mourning and misery;
 put on the splendor of glory from God forever:
wrapped in the mantle of justice from God,
 bear on your head the mitre
 that displays the glory of the eternal name.
For God will show all the earth your splendor:

you will be named by God forever
the peace of justice, the glory of God's worship.

Up, Jerusalem! stand upon the heights;
look to the east and see your children
gathered from the east and the west
at the word of the Holy One,
rejoicing that they are remembered by God.
Led away on foot by their enemies they left you:
but God will bring them back to you
borne aloft in glory as on royal thrones.
For God has commanded
that every lofty mountain be made low,
and that the age-old depths and gorges
be filled to level ground,
that Israel may advance secure in the glory of God.
The forests and every fragrant kind of tree
have overshadowed Israel at God's command;
for God is leading Israel in joy
by the light of his glory,
with his mercy and justice for company.

Action: What did the captives feel like and what did they experience as they waited to be rescued? Imagine God commanding that mountains be leveled and gorges filled in to make a smooth, easy return for them. What do they feel as they return to their homeland, thanking God that they are free at last?

Acknowledge: As you process this scene, notice what is happening in you. What thought or feeling resonates with you? What part of the passage is speaking to you? Read the passage a second time.

Relate: Turn to God and share with him what is on your heart. Think of it this way: You are watching the captives return when you notice that someone standing next to you. You realize that God is with you, and he too is watching the scene. After watching for a while, turn and look at

God. Let him look at you. Talk to him about what you noticed, thought, or felt.

Receive: What was in God's heart when his Spirit commanded the Prophet Baruch to write this passage? What is in God's heart for you? Receive whatever it is that God wants to give you — his thoughts, feelings, and desires. Read the passage a third time, or perhaps just the part that you feel most drawn to. As you do, focus on God and let him speak to you, or just quietly receive what he wants to give you.

Respond: Now answer him again. Respond to what you have received. Just be with the Lord and savor his loving presence for a minute or two before moving on.

SUGGESTIONS FOR JOURNALING

1. While imagining the scene, what stood out to me was …
2. I experienced a sense of captivity, a powerlessness and hopelessness, when …
3. When God entered the scene, I felt …
4. I sensed God communicating to me …
5. I have felt like a captive when …
6. I find the most joy when …

After you've journaled, close with a brief conversation giving thanks to God for your prayer experience. Then pray an Our Father.

December 14 — Saturday
Saturday of the Second Week of Advent

I love the Saturday review. It gives me a chance to take a break from meditating and to savor and chew on all the blessings that God has already given me. I also use Saturday to write down the biggest blessing of the week (not necessarily a prayer experience) and add that to my gratitude jar to review at the end of the year. In addition to reviewing your prayer times, you can also sift your experiences. You can look for the biggest blessing, the biggest challenge, where you saw Jesus, and a time when you were Jesus to another person. These questions also make good content for an examination of conscience at the end of each day.

Some people have told me that they are disappointed not to have a Scripture meditation on Saturdays. You can always do a Scripture meditation today. Feel free to go back and meditate on one of your favorite passages from the previous week. Alternatively, you can take the passage that was the hardest to pray with and do that one over again. When I am on silent retreat, my director often focuses on my least-fruitful prayer time. I usually find that the place of most resistance becomes the place of greatest progress. Feel free on Saturdays to pray however the Spirit as moving you. But be sure to ask the Holy Spirit for guidance and don't be afraid to follow where he leads you.

REVIEW

Preparation: *Come, Holy Spirit, enlighten the eyes of my heart.* Call to mind God's loving care for you and spend the first minute of your prayer just resting in the free, unearned gift of loving and being loved. Let gratitude rise in your heart.

Grace of the Day: What is the desire of your heart? Try to notice what you most deeply desire. Then share it with God in your own words, being confident that he loves you and wants to give you every blessing.

Week in Review: Flip back through your past week's journal entries. As you do, notice what emerged in the conversation. Here are some questions to help you:

1. Where did I notice God, and what was he doing or saying?
2. How did I respond to what God was doing?
3. I really struggled with …
4. Prayer really seemed to click when …
5. I'm grateful for …
6. Now at the end of this Second Week of Advent, what new meaning or purpose is emerging from your Advent pilgrimage? Perhaps go back and look at your very first day's prayer time.
7. What one image of God's loving presence sticks with me most strongly?

Conclude by conversing with God about your week. Acknowledge what you have been experiencing. Relate it to him. Receive what he wants to give you. Respond to him. Then savor that image of God's loving presence and rest there for a minute or two. Close with an Our Father.

Week Three

Making Prayer Happen When You Get Busy

Half an hour's meditation each day is essential, except when you are busy. Then a full hour is needed.

— *St. Francis de Sales*

It seems that my Advent always follows the same pattern. The first week or two, I find the season to be surprisingly enjoyable. I remark that I don't feel rushed this year and I look forward, finally, to a peaceful and prayerful Christmas. Then everything hits at once — Christmas cards start to pile up, time runs short, I realize that I haven't sent any cards yet, I haven't bought gifts, and now last-minute planning for the Christmas season is upon me. My general habit is to freak out, get angry, and mutter under my breath, "I hate this season. Bah humbug!"

One year when I became so overwhelmed, I quit trying at all. I just sat in my prayer space and prayed a full, solid holy hour. I may have gone a few minutes over the hour; since I wasn't going to catch up, what difference did it make? Then I wandered over to the office and, to my surprise, accomplished far more than I ever thought possible. This is the paradox of prayer. When I focus on the work, instead of God, the work piles up. When I focus on God, instead of the work, the work gets done.

This is why I encourage you not to try to catch up if you miss a day. Or a week. Or are finally opening the book for the first time. *Oriens* shouldn't be yet another thing that piles up. Rather, I want you to see it as an invitation to quiet time with the Lord. When you approach it with the right attitude, you never really "fall behind" on *Oriens*.

One of the Devil's most successful temptations is to distract people for a day or two, so they don't remember to pick up *Oriens*. Then when they finally remember to pray, the enemy whispers, "Oh well, you failed. You might as well give up now. You could try again next year." You wouldn't believe how many people fall for this little trick. There's also the daily trick: "I only have a few minutes now, so instead of praying I'll wait until later when I can pray it better." And of course, later never comes.

If you do fall a few days behind, do this: Read the Grace of the Week for the week you are on. Then turn to today's meditation and pray for today. You're all caught up! Any prayer time in a day, however small, is a victory. Even just opening the book before bed and reading the Scripture passage for that day is a victory. We are on a prayer pilgrimage. If you just keep walking, even baby steps will eventually get you to your destination.

That having been said, the more you are able to open the book each day, the more you will benefit from the pilgrimage. Our conversation with God accumulates over time. As you pray and journal regularly, you begin to notice themes emerging. There are ways and places where you experience God's love, and also places of struggle, doubt, and resistance. Be patient with your resistance, as God is patient with you. But also challenge yourself to say yes more fully, as Mary and Joseph did.

Grace of the Week: God has a plan to restore creation and undo the effects of sin. We need a Savior, and God has just the thing. Pray for the grace of a deepening desire for God and a deeper awareness of Emmanuel, God with us, in your life today.

December 15 — Sunday
Third Sunday of Advent

Preparation: *Come, Holy Spirit, enlighten the eyes of my heart.* Be present to the God who is always present to you. Call to mind his loving care for you and spend the first minute of your prayer just resting in the free, unearned gift of loving and being loved. Let gratitude rise in your heart.

Set the Scene: Ask God in your own words for a deeper desire for Him and a deeper awareness of Emmanuel, God with us, in your life today. Read the passage for the first time and set the scene in your mind. John was clothed in camel's hair and ate locusts and wild honey. He is out in the wilderness preaching repentance. Crowds are gathering along the bank of the Jordan River to be baptized by him. Spend a few minutes building the scene in your imagination. What does the wilderness look like, feel like, smell like? Picture the mass of people coming to John to repent of their sins.

LUKE 3:10–18 (LECTIONARY)

The crowds asked John the Baptist, "What should we do?" He said to them in reply, "Whoever has two cloaks should share with the person who has none. And whoever has food should do likewise." Even tax collectors came to be baptized and they said to him, "Teacher, what should we do?" He answered them, "Stop collecting more than what is prescribed." Soldiers also asked him, "And what is it that we should do?" He told them, "Do not practice extortion, do not falsely accuse anyone, and be satisfied with your wages."

Now the people were filled with expectation, and all were asking in their hearts whether John might be the Christ. John answered them all, saying, "I am baptizing you with water, but one mightier than I is coming. I am not worthy to loosen the thongs of his sandals. He will baptize you with the Holy Spirit and fire. His winnowing fan is in his hand to clear his threshing floor and to gath-

er the wheat into his barn, but the chaff he will burn with unquenchable fire." Exhorting them in many other ways, he preached good news to the people.

Action: John isn't sharing secret knowledge or giving the people complicated tasks. He's simply calling them back to honesty, generosity, and treating others fairly. We know right from wrong; we just find excuses to do what we know is wrong. What might John say to you? Read the passage a second time.

Acknowledge: Place yourself in the scene. The "one mightier than I" is somewhere in the crowd. Scan the crowd; do you notice him anywhere? What strikes you about the Christ? What is emerging inside of you as you are called to repentance and expect the coming Messiah? Notice your strongest thought, feeling, or desire.

Relate: The long-awaited Messiah is next to you, standing or sitting with you in the scene. He has come here for you. How does that make you feel? Share with him what is on your heart. Let him look at you with love. How does he respond?

Receive: Read the passage a third time. Receive whatever is in God's heart for you — his thoughts, feelings, desires.

Respond: Now answer him back again. Just be with the Lord for a minute or two before moving on.

SUGGESTIONS FOR JOURNALING
1. While imagining the scene, what stood out to me was …
2. I feel called to repent of …
3. When Jesus entered the scene, I felt …
4. I sensed God communicating to me …
5. I feel God calling me to a new way of thinking or acting …

After you've journaled, close with a brief conversation, giving thanks to God for your prayer experience. Then pray an Our Father.

December 16 — Monday
Monday of the Third Week of Advent

Preparation: *Come, Holy Spirit, enlighten the eyes of my heart.* Be present to the God who is always present to you. Call to mind his loving care for you and spend the first minute of your prayer just resting in the free, unearned gift of loving and being loved. Let gratitude rise in your heart.

Set the Scene: Ask God in your own words for a deeper desire for him and a deeper awareness of Emmanuel, God with us, in your life today. Numbers 22–24 covers the episode of Balaam, a seer and shaman. He is paid by the Moabites to curse the Israelites (shamans were commonly paid to bless their clients and curse their clients' enemies). Balaam, who "hears what God says, and knows what the Most High knows," cannot help but bless the Israelites. Picture a pagan shaman standing on a height, the Moabite prince and warriors with him, as he utters the following words.

NUMBERS 24:2–7, 15–17A (LECTIONARY)
When Balaam raised his eyes and saw Israel encamped, tribe by tribe, the spirit of God came upon him, and he gave voice to his oracle:

> *The utterance of Balaam, son of Beor,*
> *the utterance of a man whose eye is true,*
> *The utterance of one who hears what God says,*
> *and knows what the Most High knows,*
> *Of one who sees what the Almighty sees,*
> *enraptured, and with eyes unveiled:*
> *How goodly are your tents, O Jacob;*
> *your encampments, O Israel!*
> *They are like gardens beside a stream,*
> *like the cedars planted by the* Lord.

His wells shall yield free-flowing waters,
he shall have the sea within reach;
His king shall rise higher,
and his royalty shall be exalted.

Then Balaam gave voice to his oracle:

The utterance of Balaam, son of Beor,
the utterance of the man whose eye is true,
The utterance of one who hears what God says,
and knows what the Most High knows,
Of one who sees what the Almighty sees,
enraptured, and with eyes unveiled.
I see him, though not now;
I behold him, though not near:
A star shall advance from Jacob,
and a staff shall rise from Israel.

Action: Formidable forces are gathered against God's ragtag people, but the Lord will cast down the mighty from their thrones and lift up the lowly. Earthly kings appear far more rich and powerful than God's humble Anointed One, yet his kingdom will be established forever. Read the passage a second time.

Acknowledge: When have you trusted earthly powers over God's humble Anointed One? What "formidable forces" are gathered against you, seeking to curse you but to no avail, because God has blessed you? Notice your strongest thought, feeling, or desire.

Relate: When have you felt powerless against the forces of this world? Do you trust in God's plan to exult you and use you as a blessing for others? Share with God what is on your heart. Let him look at you with love. How does he respond?

Receive: Read the passage a third time. Receive whatever is in God's heart for you — his thoughts, feelings, desires, especially the words of blessing that he has already spoken over your life, and the blessing that he is preparing for you this Christmas season.

Respond: Now answer him back again. Receive his blessing. Be with the Lord for a few minutes before moving on.

SUGGESTIONS FOR JOURNALING

1. While imagining the scene, what stood out to me was …
2. I feel called to repent of …
3. I was lowly and God raised me up when …
4. The blessing that God has spoken over my life is …
5. God desires to bless me with …
6. What does it mean to receive God's blessing?

After you've journaled, close with a brief conversation, giving thanks to God for your prayer experience. Then pray an Our Father.

December 17 — Tuesday
Countdown to Christmas: Nine

O Wisdom of our God Most High,
guiding creation with power and love:
come to teach us the path of knowledge!

Nine days before Christmas, the Advent season switches gears. The lectionary turns to readings from the Gospel passages that immediately precede the birth of Jesus. Each day is assigned a special "O antiphon," a poetic invocation that draws on Old Testament prophecies to name who the coming Messiah is and what he will do. We will pray with the daily lectionary readings now until Christmas. These Gospel passages from Matthew and Luke will be familiar to you; perhaps you even prayed with them last year. As you pray with them again you will begin to see the genius of the liturgical year. God is, as Saint Augustine said, "Ever ancient, ever new." You have grown since last year's conversation with God. God will remind you of things from the past, but also guide you to new insights and experiences. Let's see what God has in store for us this year.

Preparation: *Come, Holy Spirit, enlighten the eyes of my heart.* Be present to the God who is always present to you. Call to mind his loving care for you and spend the first minute of your prayer just resting in the free, unearned gift of loving and being loved. Let gratitude rise in your heart.

Lectio: Ask God in your own words for a deeper desire for God's Wisdom who is Emmanuel, God with us, to teach you the path of knowledge. Read the passage slowly and prayerfully. Underline the names that you recognize as you go along.

MATTHEW 1:1–17 (LECTIONARY)

The book of the genealogy of Jesus Christ, the son of David, the son of Abraham.

Abraham became the father of Isaac, Isaac the father of Jacob, Jacob the father of Judah and his brothers. Judah became the father of Perez and Zerah, whose mother was Tamar. Perez became the father of Hezron, Hezron the father of Ram, Ram the father of Amminadab. Amminadab became the father of Nahshon, Nahshon the father of Salmon, Salmon the father of Boaz, whose mother was Rahab. Boaz became the father of Obed, whose mother was Ruth. Obed became the father of Jesse, Jesse the father of David the king.

David became the father of Solomon, whose mother had been the wife of Uriah. Solomon became the father of Rehoboam, Rehoboam the father of Abijah, Abijah the father of Asaph. Asaph became the father of Jehoshaphat, Jehoshaphat the father of Joram, Joram the father of Uzziah. Uzziah became the father of Jotham, Jotham the father of Ahaz, Ahaz the father of Hezekiah. Hezekiah became the father of Manasseh, Manasseh the father of Amos, Amos the father of Josiah. Josiah became the father of Jechoniah and his brothers at the time of the Babylonian exile.

After the Babylonian exile, Jechoniah became the father of Shealtiel, Shealtiel the father of Zerubbabel, Zerubbabel the father of Abiud. Abiud became the father of Eliakim, Eliakim the father of Azor, Azor the father of Zadok. Zadok became the father of Achim, Achim the father of Eliud, Eliud the father of Eleazar. Eleazar became the father of Matthan, Matthan the father of Jacob, Jacob the father of Joseph, the husband of Mary. Of her was born Jesus who is called the Christ.

Thus the total number of generations from Abraham to David is fourteen generations; from David to the Babylonian exile, fourteen generations; from the Babylonian exile to the Christ, fourteen generations.

Meditatio: We often roll our eyes at the biblical genealogy because of the unpronounceable names. But these were real people who really lived. You may not know all these names, but God knows every single person on this list, and they are all precious to him. The remains of each one are buried somewhere here on earth, and God knows the resting place of them all. Some of them were famous saints and others were rather infamous. The lineage of the Messiah is just as messy as your family history and mine (read Genesis 38 if you doubt this). Yet each person is part of the unbroken chain of ancestors that would give birth to the Son of God. Each one was chosen by God, and each person was necessary and important. All along, God was guiding creation with power and love. What does your bloodline look like? How might God be using you, and other ordinary people, to play a part in his extraordinary plans? Reflect for a few minutes, then read the passage again slowly, or just skim it and focus on whichever part spoke to you.

Oratio: In what ways is your family of origin messy? We often have pieces of our own history that are difficult, embarrassing, or hard to accept. But God willed, or allowed, both the good and the bad. These pieces contributed to who you are today. Speak to God what is on your heart and mind. There's no need to hide anything, as he knows it all. Be completely honest with him.

Contemplatio: Open your heart to receive what God wants to give you. Your life is a precious link in the chain of humanity. You are necessary, and you have a part to play not only in the lives around you, but also in the lives that will come after you. Read the passage (or skim it) for a third time. This time receive whatever God wants to show you or give you: a word, an image, a thought, or a new perspective. Perhaps he just wants to give you his peaceful assurance. God is with you in this ordinary moment. Rest in and savor his love for you.

SUGGESTIONS FOR JOURNALING
1. I see God's hand in my own personal history when …

2. Because of my family or past, I struggle with …
3. I sensed that God communicating to me …
4. I ended prayer wanting …
5. Optional: Write out your own genealogy after the style of this Scripture passage. Spend time praying for each of your ancestors.

After you've journaled, close with a brief conversation of thanksgiving to God for today's prayer time. Then pray an Our Father.

December 18 — Wednesday
Countdown to Christmas: Eight

O Leader of the House of Israel,
giver of the Law of Moses on Sinai:
come to rescue us with your mighty power!

Preparation: *Come, Holy Spirit, enlighten the eyes of my heart.* Be present to the God who is always present to you. Call to mind his loving care for you and spend the first minute of your prayer just resting in the free, unearned gift of loving and being loved. Let gratitude rise in your heart.

Set the Scene: Ask God in your own words for a deeper desire for the Leader and giver of the law who is Emmanuel, God with us, to rescue you with his mighty power. Read the passage. The betrothal of Mary and Joseph was a legal marriage. In accordance with the traditions of the time, young people married early and then prepared to live together. Joseph would have been preparing a place for his wife at his father's house. Picture the progress of this construction project. Where was Joseph sleeping? Use your imagination to set the scene.

MATTHEW 1:18–25 (LECTIONARY)

This is how the birth of Jesus Christ came about. When his mother Mary was betrothed to Joseph, but before they lived together, she was found with child through the Holy Spirit. Joseph her husband, since he was a righteous man, yet unwilling to expose her to shame, decided to divorce her quietly. Such was his intention when, behold, the angel of the Lord appeared to him in a dream and said, "Joseph, son of David, do not be afraid to take Mary your wife into your home. For it is through the Holy Spirit that this child has been conceived in her. She will bear a son and you are to name him Jesus, because he will save his people from their sins." All this took place to fulfill what the Lord had said through the prophet: Behold, the virgin shall be with child and bear a son, and they shall name him Emmanuel, which means "God is with us." When Joseph awoke, he did as the angel of the Lord had commanded him and took his wife into his home. He had no relations with her until she bore a son, and he named him Jesus.

Action: Adultery was not only a sin, but it was also a crime, punishable by stoning to death. "Divorcing her quietly" would mean not denouncing her as an adulteress. It would mean, in essence, that the whole town thought Joseph was a deadbeat dad who had got his wife pregnant and then refused to live with her. Joseph is willing to sacrifice his own reputation in order to save his wife from humiliation. It was God who gave the law that put Joseph in this predicament. Yet God will also show him a way through. God sees Joseph's willingness to sacrifice for his wife and invites him to a different form of sacrifice. What did it mean to Joseph to hear "God is with us" in his difficult situation? What did Joseph experience through this dream? What did he think or feel? How did he act on the new information?

Acknowledge: Read the passage again, and pay attention to your own heart. When have you been called to sacrifice? When has the presence of God helped you through a difficult conundrum? What does this passage stir in your heart? Notice your strongest thought, feeling, or desire.

Relate: Speak to God about what is on your heart. Let him look at you with love. How does he respond?

Receive: Read the passage a third time. This time, receive whatever is in God's heart for you — his thoughts, feelings, desires.

Respond: Now answer him back again. Just be with the Lord for a minute or two before moving on.

SUGGESTIONS FOR JOURNALING

1. I found God in the midst of my struggles when ...
2. My greatest fear or struggle seems to be ...
3. I sensed God communicating to me ...
4. I feel peace when ...
5. God's love is inviting me to a new way of seeing, thinking, or acting today, as Christmas is now just one week away ...

After you've journaled, close with a brief conversation of thanksgiving to God for today's prayer time. Then pray an Our Father.

December 19 — Thursday
Countdown to Christmas: Seven

O Root of Jesse's stem,
sign of God's love for all his people:
come to save us without delay!

Preparation: *Come, Holy Spirit, enlighten the eyes of my heart.* Be present to the God who is always present to you. Call to mind his loving care for you and spend the first minute of your prayer just resting in the free, unearned gift of loving and being loved. Let gratitude rise in your heart.

Set the Scene: Ask God in your own words for a deeper desire for the Root of Jesse's stem who is Emmanuel, God with us, to save you without delay. Read the passage. As you do, set the scene in your mind. We see an old priest going about his daily duties. What does the Temple look like? What does the angel look like? Picture the people outside waiting for Zechariah to emerge from the smoky, incense-filled Temple.

LUKE 1:5–25 (LECTIONARY)
In the days of Herod, King of Judea, there was a priest named Zechariah of the priestly division of Abijah; his wife was from the daughters of Aaron, and her name was Elizabeth. Both were righteous in the eyes of God, observing all the commandments and ordinances of the Lord blamelessly. But they had no child, because Elizabeth was barren and both were advanced in years.

Once when he was serving as priest in his division's turn before God, according to the practice of the priestly service, he was chosen by lot to enter the sanctuary of the Lord to burn incense. Then, when the whole assembly of the people was praying outside at the hour of the incense offering, the angel of the Lord appeared to him, standing at the right of the altar of incense. Zechariah was troubled by what he saw, and fear came upon him.

But the angel said to him, "Do not be afraid, Zechariah, because your prayer has been heard. Your wife Elizabeth will bear you a son, and you shall name him John. And you will have joy and gladness, and many will rejoice at his birth, for he will be great in the sight of the Lord. He will drink neither wine nor strong drink. He will be filled with the Holy Spirit even from his mother's womb, and he will turn many of the children of Israel to the Lord their God. He will go before him in the spirit and power of Elijah to turn the hearts of fathers toward children and the disobedient to the understanding of the righteous, to prepare a people fit for the Lord."

Then Zechariah said to the angel, "How shall I know this? For I am an old man, and my wife is advanced in years." And the angel said to him in reply, "I am Gabriel, who stand before God. I was sent to speak to you and to announce to you this good news. But now you will be speechless and unable to talk until the day these things take place, because you did not believe my words, which will be fulfilled at their proper time." Meanwhile the people were waiting for Zechariah and were amazed that he stayed so long in the sanctuary. But when he came out, he was unable to speak to them, and they realized that he had seen a vision in the sanctuary. He was gesturing to them but remained mute.

Then, when his days of ministry were completed, he went home.

After this time his wife Elizabeth conceived, and she went into seclusion for five months, saying, "So has the Lord done for me at a time when he has seen fit to take away my disgrace before others."

Action: Today's antiphon is drawn from Isaiah 11:1–10. King David's line had long ago been "cut off" from royal power. But God would be raising up a new shoot from the "stump of Jesse" (King David's father), and "his dwelling shall be glorious" (v. 10). In a similar way, Zechariah and Elizabeth have long given up the dream of having their own child. Even though Zechariah is ministering in the Temple, the last thing he expects is for an angel to emerge from the clouds of incense. Even less is he prepared for the Good News that the angel brings. What does he think or feel when the angel unexpectedly appears to him? How does he feel when he walks out of the Temple? How does Elizabeth feel when her husband returns home from his priestly duties, having lost the ability to speak?

Acknowledge: Read the passage a second time and play the scene forward in your mind. This time, notice what is going on inside of you. Do you sometimes doubt that God is present or will speak to you in a way that you can understand? Is there a particular word, phrase, or moment that jumps out at you from this reading? What thoughts or feelings are stirred up by this reading? What is the desire of your heart?

Relate: Speak to God about the desires of your heart. Do you believe that he is listening and will answer your prayers? Let him look at you with love. How does he respond?

Receive: Read the passage a third time and receive whatever is in God's heart for you — his thoughts, feelings, desires, his Good News for you. Do you accept that God has done good things in your life and will continue to bless you with even more blessings?

Respond: Respond to whatever God is giving you. Zechariah continued his priestly duties with a new sense that God was with him and was listening to him. Savor God's attentive presence with you for a few minutes before moving on.

SUGGESTIONS FOR JOURNALING
1. The thing that spoke to me most was …
2. I felt God stirring up a desire for …

3. I have a hard time trusting when …
4. My greatest fear or struggle seems to be …
5. I sensed God was with me and wanted me to know …

After you've journaled, close with a brief conversation giving thanks to God for your prayer experience. Then pray an Our Father.

December 20 — Friday
Countdown to Christmas: Six

O Key of David,
opening the gates of God's eternal Kingdom:
come and free the prisoners of darkness!

Preparation: *Come, Holy Spirit, enlighten the eyes of my heart.* Be present to the God who is always present to you. Call to mind his loving care for you and spend the first minute of your prayer just resting in the free, unearned gift of loving and being loved. Let gratitude rise in your heart.

Set the Scene: Ask God for a deeper desire that the Key of David might open the gates of heaven to you, that heavenly light will free you from the prison of darkness. Read the passage through. Tradition usually sets the Annunciation at Mary's home in Nazareth. What time of day was it? Perhaps Mary has paused from her chores for a little prayer time. Use your imagination to set the scene.

LUKE 1:26–38 (LECTIONARY)
In the sixth month, the angel Gabriel was sent from God to a town of Galilee called Nazareth, to a virgin betrothed to a man named Joseph, of the house of David, and the virgin's name was Mary. And coming to her, he said, "Hail, full of grace! The Lord is with you." But she was greatly troubled at what was said and pondered what sort of greeting this might be. Then the angel said to her, "Do not be afraid, Mary, for you have found favor with God. Behold, you will conceive in your womb and bear a son, and you shall name him Jesus. He will be great and will be called Son of the Most High, and the Lord God will give

him the throne of David his father, and he will rule over the house of Jacob forever, and of his Kingdom there will be no end."

But Mary said to the angel," How can this be, since I have no relations with a man?" And the angel said to her in reply, "The Holy Spirit will come upon you, and the power of the Most High will overshadow you. Therefore the child to be born will be called holy, the Son of God. And behold, Elizabeth, your relative, has also conceived a son in her old age, and this is the sixth month for her who was called barren; for nothing will be impossible for God."

Mary said, "Behold, I am the handmaid of the Lord. May it be done to me according to your word." Then the angel departed from her.

Action: Today's O antiphon takes the key of David (see Is 22:22) in two different directions: It will open the kingdom of heaven that was closed by Eve's sin, and it will unlock the prisoners who have been kept in darkness by that same sin. But the key doesn't have the power to unlock Mary's womb; only she can do that. All of creation, groaning under the sentence of sin, awaits her answer with bated breath. What will she say? Will we finally have the long-awaited Savior that God has promised us?

Acknowledge: Why is this virgin greatly troubled at the angel's words? What is in her heart at this moment? What does her yes feel like for her? Read the passage a second time. Notice what is going on inside of you. Do you sometimes have a hard time accepting God's plans for your life? Is God waiting for you to "unlock" your heart to him?

Relate: Speak to Mary about your thoughts and feelings. Together with her, turn to God in prayer. Share what is on your heart with complete honesty. Question God, as Mary questioned the angel. Don't hide your feelings from God.

Receive: Read the passage a third time. Receive whatever is in God's heart for you — his thoughts, feelings, desires. He prepared the way for centuries and sent his angel to Mary for you, so that you could receive salvation and new life. What more does he want to give you? If you have a hard time receiving, ask Mary to show you how to receive.

Respond: God wants to dwell in your heart as he dwelt in the womb of Mary. Cherish the gift of God's love, not only for you and with you, but even within you. Converse with God in your heart. Then just be with the Lord and with Mary for a minute or two before moving on.

SUGGESTIONS FOR JOURNALING

1. My heart is troubled by …
2. How have I responded when God's plans interrupted my plans?
3. God's presence feels like …
4. I sensed that God was with me and wanted me to know …
5. I ended prayer wanting …

After you've journaled, close with a brief conversation with God giving thanks for your prayer experience. Then pray a Hail Mary.

December 21 — Saturday
Countdown to Christmas: Five

O Emmanuel, our King and Giver of Law:
Come to save us, Lord our God!

Preparation: *Come, Holy Spirit, enlighten the eyes of my heart.* Be present to the God who is always present to you. Call to mind his loving care for you and spend the first minute of your prayer just resting in the free, unearned gift of loving and being loved. Let gratitude rise in your heart.

Set the Scene: Ask in your own words that the Emmanuel, God with us, will be your King and save you by his just law. Read the passage through and picture the scene in your imagination. Tradition identifies this location as a town called Ein Karem, a hill town about five miles to the west of Jerusalem and about ninety miles from Nazareth. Elizabeth is already six months pregnant. Mary hasn't started to show yet.

LUKE 1:39–45 (LECTIONARY)
Mary set out in those days and traveled to the hill country in haste to a town of Judah, where she entered the house of Zechariah and greeted Elizabeth. When Elizabeth heard Mary's greeting, the infant leaped in her womb, and Elizabeth, filled with the Holy Spirit, cried out in a loud voice and said, "Most blessed are you among women, and blessed is the fruit of your womb. And how does this happen to me, that the mother of my Lord should come to me? For at the moment the sound of your greeting reached my ears, the infant in my womb leaped for joy. Blessed are you who believed that what was spoken to you by the Lord would be fulfilled."

Action: Emmanuel means "God with us" (Is 7:14). How was God with Mary on her journey to visit Elizabeth? What does Elizabeth feel in the presence of her infant Lord? What does Mary feel as Elizabeth rejoices in her pregnancy?

Acknowledge: The same Lord who was present in the womb of Mary is also with you in your prayer time. Read the passage a second time and play the scene forward in your mind. Christmas is a busy time for visiting and receiving visitors. Do your visitors bring the presence of Jesus to your home, or do they bring worries of being judged for a messy home? When you visit others, how do you bring Jesus with you to their home? When did you leap for joy at God's presence in your life?

Relate: Let your thoughts and feelings rise to the surface. Speak to God what is in your heart.

Receive: Read the passage a third time. How does God the Father view this scene? How does he gaze upon your visits and visitors? Receive whatever is in God's heart for you — his thoughts, feelings, desires.

Respond: Converse with God in your heart. Then just savor the presence of Jesus for a minute or two before moving on.

SUGGESTIONS FOR JOURNALING
1. My heart leaped for joy when …
2. My strongest thought, feeling, or desire was …
3. I sensed God saying to me …
4. I ended prayer wanting …
5. Is there a way I can "go in haste" to share with another the joy I am receiving through these Advent prayer times?

―――――――――――――――――――――――――――――――――――

―――――――――――――――――――――――――――――――――――

―――――――――――――――――――――――――――――――――――

―――――――――――――――――――――――――――――――――――

―――――――――――――――――――――――――――――――――――

―――――――――――――――――――――――――――――――――――

―――――――――――――――――――――――――――――――――――

―――――――――――――――――――――――――――――――――――

―――――――――――――――――――――――――――――――――――

―――――――――――――――――――――――――――――――――――

―――――――――――――――――――――――――――――――――――

―――――――――――――――――――――――――――――――――――

―――――――――――――――――――――――――――――――――――

A BRIEF REVIEW

Take a little time at the end of your prayer today and flip back through the previous week.

1. How has God been present to me in the midst of the season's busyness?
2. Is there a particular theme that is emerging on my Advent pilgrimage?
3. What helps me stay present to God throughout the day, after my prayer time is done?
4. During the final rush to Christmas, I desire most deeply …

5. The clearest and most powerful image of God's love for me has been …

Acknowledge what you have been experiencing. **Relate** it to him. **Receive** what he wants to give you. **Respond** to him. Then savor that image of God's loving presence and rest there for a minute or two. Close with an Our Father or a Hail Mary.

Week Four

Lord, When Did You Get Here? (Jn 6:25)

"Be vigilant at all times, and pray" (Lk 21:36a). Our Advent season began with these words. Holy Mother Church tells us to get ready to celebrate the coming of Christ on December 25. We are at the same time called to prepare ourselves for the Second Coming of Christ. We gaze off into the distance, eagerly scanning the horizon to catch a glimpse of the Master. Then we notice, to our surprise, that he is already here with us.

I fully expect that you have had this experience on your Advent journey. Whether in prayer time or in the moments of everyday life, Jesus continues to be Emmanuel, God with us. We think that God needs to come to us. But the truth is that our eyes must be opened to his constant, quiet, humble presence.

After one walking pilgrimage, three of us were interviewed by Relevant Radio. The host said, "It must be an amazing experience when you finally walk into the shrine after all those miles."

The pilgrims looked at each other.

"It's not like you are waiting the whole time for one big payout at the end," I said.

"You get a lot of graces and blessings along the way," said another.

"Yes, there's a great feeling of joy and relief when you finish, but the pilgrimage is about more than that," said the third pilgrim.

A walking pilgrimage is about far more than getting to the destination. You are changed by the journey. This is precisely why *Oriens* is *a pilgrimage* through Advent and Christmas. I firmly believe that the daily prayer time you have invested in is opening the eyes of your heart to the presence of Jesus alive and active in your life. Jesus has always been with us; we just didn't know how to see him.

We have three more preparation days in this Advent season. Then the Christmas celebration begins. I say it "begins" because the feast of Christmas is too big to fit into one day. For eight days we celebrate the long-awaited Radiant Dawn, the Sun of Justice and King all nations who is Christ the Lord.

Grace of the Week: Ask God for a deeper experience of the Love that is Emmanuel, God with us, that your heart may be filled with warmth and light.

December 22 — Sunday
Fourth Sunday of Advent

Countdown to Christmas: Four

O King of all nations and keystone of the Church:
come and save man, whom you formed from the dust!

Preparation: *Come, Holy Spirit, enlighten the eyes of my heart.* Be present to the God who is always present to you. Call to mind his loving care for you and spend the first minute of your prayer just resting in the free, unearned gift of loving and being loved. Let gratitude rise in your heart.

Lectio: Ask God in your own words that you might experience the joy of Emmanuel, God with us, saving you who were formed from the dust of the earth. Read the passage slowly and prayerfully. This Scripture is called the *Magnificat* (which is the first word of this passage in Latin). It is a hymn of praise to God who has been faithful to his promises from Abraham until today. This could very well be a song that the saints sing in heaven. Is there one word or phrase that you feel moved to focus on?

LUKE 1:46–56 (LECTIONARY)
Mary said: "My soul proclaims the greatness of the Lord; my spirit rejoices in God my savior, for he has looked upon his lowly servant. From this day all generations will call me blessed; the Almighty has done great things for me, and holy is his Name. He has mercy on those who fear him in every generation. He has shown the strength of his arm, and has scattered the proud in their conceit. He has cast down the mighty from their thrones and has lifted up the lowly. He has filled the hungry with good things, and the

rich he has sent away empty. He come to the help of his servant Israel for he has remembered his promise of mercy, the promise he made to our fathers, to Abraham and to his children for ever."

Mary remained with Elizabeth about three months and then returned to her home.

Meditatio: The Bible loves to remind us that "many who are first will be last, and the last will be first" (Mt 19:30). The news often carries stories of the once wealthy and powerful who are now facing justice for their misdeeds. Yet we continue to admire the wealthy and powerful and often seek to imitate them. Today's Scripture invites us to imitate the "handmaid of the Lord" whom God raised to be the "Queen of Heaven." Have you, or people you know, experienced the humbling of a divorce, financial problems, or health challenges, only to find blessing and new life on the other side? Perhaps you feel lowly and humbled, like someone who needs to be raised from the dust, and you are waiting for the King of all nations to come rescue you with the might of his arm. Reflect for a few minutes or just focus on the word or phrase that speaks to you. Then read the passage again slowly.

Oratio: Speak to God what is on your heart and mind, your thoughts, feelings, and desires. When you are done speaking, read the passage one more time.

Contemplatio: Open your heart to receive what God wants to give you. Maybe it is a thought, a word, or a sense of peace. God is with you in this ordinary moment. Rest in and savor his love for you. Be present. Be lowly.

SUGGESTIONS FOR JOURNALING
1. My favorite word or phrase was …
2. I needed to be reminded that …
3. God fulfilled his promises to me when …
4. I rejoice in God my Savior when I recall …
5. Whom can I visit, call, or reach out to with encouraging words?

After you've journaled, close with a brief conversation with God giving thanks for your prayer experience. Then close by reading today's Scripture one more time as a prayer of praise and thanksgiving.

December 23 — Monday
Countdown to Christmas: Three

O King of all nations and keystone of the Church:
come and save man, whom you formed from the dust!

Preparation: *Come, Holy Spirit, enlighten the eyes of my heart.* Be present to the God who is always present to you. Call to mind his loving care for you and spend the first minute of your prayer just resting in the free, unearned gift of loving and being loved. Let gratitude rise in your heart.

Set the Scene: Ask God in your own words that the King of all nations who is Emmanuel, God with us, will save you who were formed from the dust of the earth. It's easy to imagine Elizabeth's neighbors and relatives gathering around to celebrate the birth of a healthy baby boy. The circumcision was like a baptism party. The name *John* means "God is gracious." Set the scene in your imagination. Populate it with villagers.

LUKE 1:57–66 (LECTIONARY)
When the time arrived for Elizabeth to have her child she gave birth to a son. Her neighbors and relatives heard that the Lord had shown his great mercy toward her, and they rejoiced with her. When they came on the eighth day to circumcise the child, they were going to call him Zechariah after his father, but his mother said in reply, "No. He will be called John." But they answered her, "There is no one among your relatives who has this name." So they made signs, asking his father what he wished him to be called. He asked for a tablet and wrote, "John is his name," and all were amazed. Immediately his mouth was opened, his tongue freed, and he spoke blessing God.

Then fear came upon all their neighbors, and all these matters were discussed throughout the hill country of Judea. All who heard these things took them to heart, saying, "What, then, will this child be? For surely the hand of the Lord was with him."

Action: See the looks on the faces of the guests and their excited conversation. Zechariah is only a silent participant — imagine the look on his face as he holds his son for the first time. Imagine the look on everyone's face when suddenly he can speak again! Even though Mary isn't mentioned, she was probably in the crowd somewhere — why else would she have remained for three months with Elizabeth? Place yourself within the crowd.

Acknowledge: Read the passage a second time. After centuries of silence, God is finally moving in a big way. This little child will prepare the way for the King of all nations and keystone of the Church to come and save you. What thoughts and feelings rise in your heart?

Relate: Speak to God what is in your heart. If you have a hard time expressing yourself, maybe Zechariah can help.

Receive: Read the passage a third time and receive whatever is in God's heart for you — his thoughts, feelings, desires. Does your heavenly Father look at you like Zechariah looked at his son, John?

Respond: The hand of the Lord is with you, too. Let the Father look at you and look back at him. Just savor the joy of being your Father's child for a few minutes before moving on.

SUGGESTIONS FOR JOURNALING
1. I was surprised by …
2. Zechariah teaches me …
3. The Father seemed to be saying to me …
4. When do I feel tongue-tied, or when do I find it hard to speak to God?

5. Was there something today that I had a hard time receiving and accepting?
6. I ended prayer wanting ...

_____

_____

_____

_____

_____

_____

_____

_____

_____

_____

_____

_____

_____

_____

_____

_____

_____

After you've journaled, close with a brief conversation with God giving thanks for your prayer experience. Then pray an Our Father.

December 24 — Tuesday
Countdown to Christmas: Two

O Radiant Dawn,
splendor of eternal light, sun of justice:
come and shine on those who dwell in darkness and in the
shadow of death.

Preparation: *Come, Holy Spirit, enlighten the eyes of my heart.* Be present to the God who is always present to you. Call to mind his loving care for you and spend the first minute of your prayer just resting in the free, unearned gift of loving and being loved. Let gratitude rise in your heart.

Lectio: Ask God in your own words for the dawning of Emmanuel, God with us, that the sun of justice might shine the splendor of eternal light on us who dwell in darkness. Zechariah hasn't spoken for nine months — and now he has a lot to say! He proclaims that this child will brighten all the world and bring a freedom far greater than the Israelites experienced as they left Egypt. Read this passage slowly and prayerfully. Is there a word or phrase that speaks to you most strongly?

LUKE 1:67–79
Zechariah his father, filled with the holy Spirit, prophe-
sied, saying:

> *"Blessed be the Lord, the God of Israel,*
> *for he has visited and brought redemption to*
> *his people.*
> *He has raised up a horn for our salvation*
> *within the house of David his servant,*
> *even as he promised through the mouth of his holy*

prophets from of old:
     salvation from our enemies and from the hand
of all who hate us,
to show mercy to our fathers
     and to be mindful of his holy covenant
and of the oath he swore to Abraham our father,
         and to grant us that, rescued from the hand
of enemies, without fear we might worship him in
holiness and righteousness
     before him all our days.
And you, child, will be called prophet of the Most
High,
     for you will go before the Lord to prepare his
ways,
to give his people knowledge of salvation
     through the forgiveness of their sins,
because of the tender mercy of our God
     by which the daybreak from on high will visit us
to shine on those who sit in darkness and death's
shadow,
     to guide our feet into the path of peace."

Meditatio: O Radiant Dawn! The dawn from on high that shall break upon us. You guessed it, that is the word *oriens*. With this being the day before Christmas, it is as though the dawn is just starting to peek out over the hills. Have you felt God's light beginning to shine more brightly in these Advent days? Has God been guiding your feet into the way of peace? Read the passage again and notice the part that most speaks to your heart.

Oratio: What do you want to say to God, with the birth of his Son so close at hand? What do you most hope for or desire? Speak to God what is on your heart and mind.

Contemplatio: Read the passage one more time. Open your heart to receive what God wants to give you. God loves every child like an only child. Rest in and savor his love for you. Let the dawn from on high shine upon you. Bask in the light of God's love for a few minutes before moving on.

SUGGESTIONS FOR JOURNALING

1. I see more clearly now …
2. I more strongly desire …
3. I need patience as I wait for …
4. God's love feels like …
5. What I really want for Christmas is …

_____

_____

_____

_____

_____

_____

_____

_____

_____

_____

_____

_____

_____

_____

_____

_____

_____

_____

_____

After you've journaled, close with a brief conversation with God giving thanks for your prayer experience. Then read today's Scripture one more time as a prayer of praise and thanksgiving.

The King Is Born

The text below, taken from the Roman martyrology, presents the birth of Jesus as one would announce the birth of a king or emperor. The announcement is recited or chanted on December 24, during the celebration of the Liturgy of the Hours or before the Christmas Mass during the night.

Let us prepare our hearts to celebrate the birth of our Savior. Come, Lord Jesus, into our hearts, our families, our world!

The Twenty-fifth Day of December, when ages beyond number had run their course from the creation of the world, when God in the beginning created heaven and earth, and formed man in his own likeness;

when century upon century had passed since the Almighty set his bow in the clouds after the Great Flood, as a sign of covenant and peace; in the twenty-first century since Abraham, our father in faith, came out of Ur of the Chaldees;

in the thirteenth century since the People of Israel were led by Moses in the Exodus from Egypt; around the thousandth year since David was anointed King;

in the sixty-fifth week of the prophecy of Daniel; in the one hundred and ninety-fourth Olympiad; in the year seven hundred and fifty-two since the foundation of the City of Rome;

in the forty-second year of the reign of Caesar Octavian Augustus, the whole world being at peace,

JESUS CHRIST, eternal God and Son of the eternal Father, desiring to consecrate the world by his most loving presence, was conceived by the Holy Spirit, and when nine months had passed since his conception, was born of the Virgin Mary in Bethlehem of Judah, and was made man:

The Nativity of Our Lord Jesus Christ according to the flesh. (Appendix 1 of the *Roman Missal*, 3rd ed.)

December 25 — Wednesday
The Nativity of Our Lord Jesus Christ

Merry Christmas! For Catholics, Christmas Day is just the first day of the eight-day octave of Christmas. I tell school children that the octave of Christmas means that you have to eat Christmas treats every day for eight days. The Gloria is sung at Mass for all eight days of the octave. Several of these days are special feast days dedicated to particular saints. Celebrate Christmas by lighting your Christmas tree, putting baby Jesus in the manger of your crèche, and placing fresh, white candles in your Advent wreath. Light them when you eat your family meals, and sing a Christmas carol together each time. Today can be a busy day for many, and you may find it hard to pray. Try to make a little time at the beginning or the end of the day to cozy up in view of your Christmas tree and pray with today's readings. Keep making time for your prayer pilgrimage! We've come through Advent and have only just begun our journey through Christmas.

Preparation: *Come, Holy Spirit, enlighten the eyes of my heart.* Be present to the God who is always present to you. Call to mind his loving care for you and spend the first minute of your prayer just resting in the free, unearned gift of loving and being loved. Let gratitude rise in your heart.

Set the Scene: Pray for the grace to more deeply experience Emmanuel, God with us, in your heart today. We like to think of the Nativity as something easy, peaceful, and cozy. But our Gospel implies crowds thronging to fulfill the decree, a long journey on dusty roads with a very pregnant woman, and finding yourself homeless at the most inopportune time. Read through the Gospel to set the scene in your imagination.

LUKE 2:1–20 (LECTIONARY)
In those days a decree went out from Caesar Augustus that the whole world should be enrolled. This was the first

enrollment, when Quirinius was governor of Syria. So all went to be enrolled, each to his own town. And Joseph too went up from Galilee from the town of Nazareth to Judea, to the city of David that is called Bethlehem, because he was of the house and family of David, to be enrolled with Mary, his betrothed, who was with child. While they were there, the time came for her to have her child, and she gave birth to her firstborn son. She wrapped him in swaddling clothes and laid him in a manger, because there was no room for them in the inn.

Now there were shepherds in that region living in the fields and keeping the night watch over their flock. The angel of the Lord appeared to them and the glory of the Lord shone around them, and they were struck with great fear. The angel said to them, "Do not be afraid; for behold, I proclaim to you good news of great joy that will be for all the people. For today in the city of David a savior has been born for you who is Christ and Lord. And this will be a sign for you: you will find an infant wrapped in swaddling clothes and lying in a manger." And suddenly there was a multitude of the heavenly host with the angel, praising God and saying:

"Glory to God in the highest
  and on earth peace to those on whom his favor rests."

When the angels went away from them to heaven, the shepherds said to one another, "Let us go, then, to Bethlehem to see this thing that has taken place, which the Lord has made known to us." So they went in haste and found Mary and Joseph, and the infant lying in the manger. When they saw this, they made known the message that had been told them about this child. All who heard it were amazed by what had been told them by the shepherds. And Mary kept all these things, reflecting on them *in her heart. Then the shepherds returned, glorifying and praising God for all they had heard and seen, just as it had been told to them.*

Action: Sometimes we find ourselves trying to make a life for ourselves as world events swirl around us. Did Joseph and Mary know why they were making this journey? Did they perhaps fret about the destination and the challenge of finding housing? God provides an unorthodox, but effective, bed for his little Son. God "lifts up the lowly" by inviting humble shepherds to come and adore the newborn king. What is in Mary's heart, Joseph's heart, and the hearts of the shepherds?

Acknowledge: Where do you find yourself in this scene? Read the passage a second time. What part of the story most stirs your heart? Perhaps ask Mary to let you hold her newborn babe. What do you feel as you gaze upon the face of God?

Relate: Open your heart to the God who loves you. Speak to God from your heart, or just adore him if you cannot find the words to speak.

Receive: Read the passage a third time, or just the part that most strongly spoke to you. What is in Baby Jesus's heart for you? What does he want you to know? Receive whatever God wants to give you.

Respond: Savor the joy of holding the Son and being held by the Father for a little while, while Mary and Joseph surround you with their love and tenderness. Let God the Father gaze at you as you gaze on the face of his Son. Behold, and be held.

SUGGESTIONS FOR JOURNALING

1. The glory of the Lord shone in my Christmas celebration when ...
2. I felt God's love most strongly ...
3. Baby Jesus wanted to give me ...
4. I was surprised by ...
5. My heart rested when ...

After you've journaled, close with a brief conversation with God giving thanks for your prayer experience. Then pray an Our Father.

December 26 — Thursday
Second Day in the Octave of Christmas

SAINT STEPHEN, DEACON AND MARTYR

Stephen was one of seven men chosen to be the first deacons of the infant church (see Acts 6:1–6). They were ordained specifically to take over the Church's care for the widows, a sign that charity for the needy is an essential part of the Gospel. He did great wonders and signs and preached the Gospel with so much wisdom that his opponents were confounded. They falsely accused him of blasphemy, and a mob stoned him to death (6:8—8:1). He is the first in a long line of faithful servants who gave their lives in witness to the true King. This feast reminds us that Jesus was born into time so that Stephen, and all of us, could be born into eternity.

Preparation: *Come, Holy Spirit, enlighten the eyes of my heart.* Be present to the God who is always present to you. Call to mind his loving care for you and spend the first minute of your prayer just resting in the free, unearned gift of loving and being loved. Let gratitude rise in your heart.

Set the Scene: Ask God for the grace of a deeper sense of peace and joy in the birth of Jesus, and pray that his love will fill your heart with warmth and light. Hopefully we are still glowing with the light of the Nativity scene. We want the peace and joy of Baby Jesus to enter more deeply into our hearts. The Church has long celebrated the feast of the first martyr the day after the birthday of Jesus. Whenever the Church gives us something incongruous, such as placing a martyrdom in the heart of the Christmas octave, she gives us an opportunity to find deeper meaning and new connections within our faith. The young Christian Church has been spreading rapidly. Stephen is an effective apologist, meaning that he explains and defends our faith in Jesus Christ. He is also filled with the Holy Spirit; the "signs and wonders" the Bible mentions him working are most likely miracles of healing and exorcism. His opponents try to prove him wrong through philosophical and theological debates, but the debate only proves him more right. They resort to violence. Read the passage and use your imagination to picture the scene.

ACTS 6:8–10; 7:54–59 (LECTIONARY)

Stephen, filled with grace and power, was working great wonders and signs among the people. Certain members of the so-called Synagogue of Freedmen, Cyrenians, and Alexandrians, and people from Cilicia and Asia, came forward and debated with Stephen, but they could not withstand the wisdom and the spirit with which he spoke.

When they heard this, they were infuriated, and they ground their teeth at him. But he, filled with the Holy Spirit, looked up intently to heaven and saw the glory of God and Jesus standing at the right hand of God, and he said, "Behold, I see the heavens opened and the Son of Man standing at the right hand of God." But they cried out in a loud voice, covered their ears, and rushed upon him together. They threw him out of the city, and began to stone him. The witnesses laid down their cloaks at the feet of a young man named Saul. As they were stoning Stephen, he called out, "Lord Jesus, receive my spirit."

Action: As the whirlwind of anger and hatred unfolds around him, focus on the peace in Stephen's heart. Acts 6:15 says, "All those who sat in the Sanhedrin looked intently at him and saw that his face was like the face of an angel." The heavens are opened, and Stephen sees Jesus himself in glory. His life ends in imitation of Jesus's death on the cross. Like Jesus's own death, the death of Stephen is a story of redemption. The Saul who appears at the end of today's reading will eventually be converted to the same Faith he once persecuted. Stephen loved his enemies and prayed for those who persecuted him. Was Saul's conversion a fruit of Stephen's prayer?

Acknowledge: Read the passage a second time. Place yourself in the scene. Can you see the light of Christ reflected in Stephen's face as he is being brutally murdered? What thoughts, feelings, and desires are rising in your heart?

Relate: The same Jesus who appeared to Stephen standing at the right hand of God is now standing with you. Turn to him. Share with him honestly what is on your heart, without fear of "saying the wrong thing" or being judged. Jesus already knows what you are thinking, but he's waiting for you to turn to him.

Receive: Read the passage a third time, or just the part that spoke to you. Open your heart to what the Heart of Jesus wants to give you — a word, a phrase, or just his silent, loving presence. Spend a few minutes in the presence of the Almighty who became a little child.

Respond: You too are valuable to God, as Stephen was valuable to him. Savor the light of the Holy Spirit shining on your heart and respond to whatever God is giving you. Spend a minute or two in silent conversation before moving on.

SUGGESTIONS FOR JOURNALING
1. I never realized that …
2. I see a new connection between Christmas and the feast of Stephen …
3. My strongest thought, feeling, or desire was …
4. Jesus gave me the gift of …
5. I ended prayer with a new appreciation of the Christmas story …

After you've journaled, thank God for his presence with you and his love for you in today's prayer time. Join with Stephen and all the members of God's heavenly family as you pray an Our Father.

December 27 — Friday
Third Day in the Octave of Christmas

SAINT JOHN, APOSTLE AND EVANGELIST

Born in Bethsaida, the brother of James and a fisherman by trade, John was called to follow Jesus while mending his nets at the Sea of Galilee. Along with his brother James and fellow fisherman Peter, he was present at the Transfiguration of the Lord. At the Last Supper, he reclined at table next to Jesus. He stood at the foot of the cross as Jesus died, and Jesus entrusted his mother to John's care. He is known as the "beloved disciple." John wrote the fourth Gospel, three epistles, and the Book of Revelation. The youngest of all the apostles, he was the only one not to be martyred. Tradition holds that he was miraculously preserved from attempts to kill him and was then exiled to the island of Patmos, where he died of old age.

Preparation: *Come, Holy Spirit, enlighten the eyes of my heart.* Be present to the God who is always present to you. Call to mind his loving care for you and spend the first minute of your prayer just resting in the free, unearned gift of loving and being loved. Let gratitude rise in your heart.

Lectio: Ask God in your own words for a deeper sense of peace and joy in the birth of Jesus, that his light will shine in the dark corners of your heart and your world. Saint John is perhaps writing this passage in his later years, when doubters have come to question the eyewitness accounts of the apostles. He wants to assure his readers that their Faith is based on the truth. As you read it, picture an old man dictating these words to a scribe. He is wrinkled and bent by the years, but his eyes are young and sparkle with love and joy. He can still picture the scenes of the Gospel as if they were yesterday. Picture those scenes yourself as you read this passage.

1 JOHN 1:1–4 (LECTIONARY)

Beloved:
What was from the beginning,
what we have heard,
what we have seen with our eyes,
what we looked upon
and touched with our hands
concerns the Word of life —
for the life was made visible;
we have seen it and testify to it
and proclaim to you the eternal life
that was with the Father and was made visible to us —
what we have seen and heard
we proclaim now to you,
so that you too may have fellowship with us;
for our fellowship is with the Father
and with his Son, Jesus Christ.
We are writing this so that our joy may be complete.

Meditatio: The "beloved disciple" savors the fellowship that he has with the Father and the Son. He wants every Christian, and indeed every person, to experience this same fellowship. How has God's word of life been made visible to you on your *Oriens* pilgrimage? Have you seen God's love, felt his presence, or experienced answers to prayer? You too can join Saint John in witnessing that Jesus is alive. Read the passage again, trying to make these words your own words.

Oratio: "I am with you always, until the end of the age" (Mt 28:20), Jesus had promised Saint John. And Jesus is with you too. What thoughts, feelings, or desires arise in your heart? Can you put them into words? Speak your words to the Word of life.

Contemplatio: How does Jesus receive what is in your heart? What is in his heart for you? Read the passage a third time, and this time just bask in the fellowship you have with the Father and with his Son, Jesus Christ. Let gratitude rise in your heart, followed by a deep joy. Allow that joy to fill you for a few minutes before moving on.

SUGGESTIONS FOR JOURNALING

1. I have heard, seen, and touched the word of God for myself when ...
2. I have experienced fellowship with God when ...
3. I sometimes find myself doubting that ...
4. I was encouraged by ...
5. I ended prayer wanting ...

After you've journaled, close with a brief conversation with God giving thanks for your prayer experience. Then pray an Our Father.

December 28 — Saturday
Fourth Day in the Octave of Christmas

THE HOLY INNOCENTS, MARTYRS

"When Jesus was born in Bethlehem of Judea, in the days of King Herod, behold, magi from the east arrived in Jerusalem, saying, 'Where is the newborn king of the Jews? We saw his star at its rising and have come to do him homage'" (Mt 2:1–2). King Herod pretended to be excited, but instead planned to let the magi find the child so that he could murder him. He had already murdered several of his sons and family members in order to protect his throne. The magi were warned in a dream and departed by another way. "When Herod realized that he had been deceived by the magi, he became furious. He ordered the massacre of all the boys in Bethlehem and its vicinity two years old and under, in accordance with the time he had ascertained from the magi" (Mt 2:16). The Gospel of Matthew depicts Jesus as re-living the history of the nation of Israel. Jews would have recognized Pharaoh ordering the drowning of all the Hebrew baby boys in the Nile River (see Ex 1:22). Christians have treated these tiny innocent victims as martyrs who, by their death for Jesus, won the victory of eternal life.

> With the mouths of babes and infants.
>   You have established a bulwark against your foes,
> to silence enemy and avenger. (Psalm 8:3)

Preparation: *Come, Holy Spirit, enlighten the eyes of my heart.* Call to mind God's loving care for you and spend the first minute of your prayer just resting in the free, unearned gift of loving and being loved. Let gratitude rise in your heart.

Grace for the Day: What is the desire of your heart? Try to notice what you most deeply desire. Then share it with God in your own words, being confident that he loves you and wants to give you every blessing.

Week in Review: Flip back through your past week's journal entries. As you do, notice what emerged in the conversation. Here are some questions to help you:

1. Where did I notice God, and what was he doing or saying?
2. How did I respond to what God was doing?
3. I felt God's love most strongly when …
4. I found myself struggling with …
5. I'm grateful for …

_____

_____

_____

_____

_____

_____

_____

_____

Now go back to your journal entries from the First Sunday of Advent and then the last few Saturday reviews.

1. What did I desire as I began this journey? Have those desires grown or changed in some way?
2. Do I notice a particular theme that has been emerging on my Advent pilgrimage?
3. Do I have recurring fears or struggles that Jesus is wanting to address with me?
4. This Christmas, God has given me the gift of …
5. How has this Advent journey changed me?
6. My strongest sense, image, moment, or experience of God's loving presence was …

_____

_____

_____

_____

_____

Acknowledge what you have been experiencing. **Relate** it to him. **Receive** what he wants to give you. **Respond** to him. Then savor that image of God's loving presence and rest there for a minute or two. Close with an Our Father.

Week Five

Week Five

A Feast Fit for a King

The feast of Christmas is too big to fit into one day. For eight days we celebrate the long-awaited Radiant Dawn, the Sun of Justice and King all nations who is Christ the Lord. The octave always includes the feast of the Holy Family and ends with the solemnity of Mary, the Mother of God, on January 1. The twelve days of Christmas run until Epiphany, traditionally celebrated on January 6. There is another forty-day period that ends on the feast of the Presentation, February 2. Christmas is more than one feast, as the gift of Emmanuel is so much more than just a single gift. Throughout these days I hope you can continue to marvel at the many facets of the mystery of the Incarnation.

Maybe you had the best of intentions but just forgot to pick up this book. That's OK! You can start praying again any time. Pilgrimages are never just a smooth road. On my five-day walking pilgrimages, the middle day is usually a Wednesday, and it is often the most challenging day for pilgrims. You might find reasons to give up, excuses not to pray, or you might say things like "I'll just try again next year." Just because it wasn't the pilgrimage that you wanted doesn't mean that you've missed out on the journey that God planned for you. Do not be discouraged when you encounter various forms of resistance. If praying was hard for you, if you were tempted to give up, if you faced criticism from friends or family members, if you felt discouraged, or that you were "no good at praying" … good! Resistance is part of the journey. Overcoming resistance is an important part of growth in any area of our lives. If you encounter resistance, it is a sign that you are on the right road. Keep walking!

Do not be discouraged either if your *Oriens* pilgrimage hasn't yet been what you were perhaps expecting or hoping it would be. I once went on a pilgrimage to the Holy Land, and we visited the Sea of Galilee for a five-day retreat. It was the most dry and difficult retreat I've ever had. I got no fruit from any of the prayer times until after the retreat had technically ended. After the final prayer time, I finally vented to God how upset I was. It was then that God revealed his presence throughout the entire retreat. While it wasn't the retreat that I wanted, I have never forgotten the lessons God gave me.

Remember that prayer is not about filling pages of a journal with amazing insights or experiences. You shouldn't compare your retreat with anyone else's. If you are open to an encounter, then God will come and meet you. If you have spent any quality time with God in these days, your pilgrim journey has been a blessing. We still have more than half our pilgrimage ahead of us. So, keep walking and let's see what awaits us around the next corner.

Grace of the Week: We continue to celebrate the octave of Christmas. Our readings this week will be drawn from the daily Mass readings or the Scriptures for each feast day. Pray for a deeper sense of peace and joy in the birth of Jesus, and pray that his light will shine in the dark corners of your heart and your world.

December 29 — Sunday
The Holy Family of Jesus, Mary, and Joseph

Preparation: *Come, Holy Spirit, enlighten the eyes of my heart.* Be present to the God who is always present to you. Call to mind his loving care for you and spend the first minute of your prayer just resting in the free, unearned gift of loving and being loved. Let gratitude rise in your heart.

Set the Scene: Ask God in your own words for a deeper sense of joy and peace in the birth of Jesus, that his light will shine in the dark corners of your heart and your world. Read the passage through. The reading for today's feast day is the "finding of Jesus in the Temple" — baby Jesus sure grew up quickly! This passage is the only scriptural reference to Jesus's life between his infancy and the beginning of his public ministry. We don't often see this passage in the light of the Christmas story. Let's dig into it and see what it can tell us about Jesus's birth. As you read it, set the scene in your mind. Picture the chaos as many pilgrims arrive in Jerusalem (not unlike the census years earlier). At twelve years of age, Jesus is now mature enough to participate in this yearly custom for the first time. He probably spent a lot of time with the other boys his age, as well as relatives and acquaintances of his parents. So, his parents didn't notice his absence at first. We often think of the Holy Family posing in the manger scene, a perfect child and perfect parents. But apparently, even the Holy Family struggled sometimes.

LUKE 2:41–52 (LECTIONARY)

Each year Jesus' parents went to Jerusalem for the feast of Passover, and when he was twelve years old, they went up according to festival custom. After they had completed its days, as they were returning, the boy Jesus remained behind in Jerusalem, but his parents did not know it. Thinking that he was in the caravan, they journeyed for a day and looked for him among their relatives and acquain-

tances, but not finding him, they returned to Jerusalem to look for him. After three days they found him in the temple, sitting in the midst of the teachers, listening to them and asking them questions, and all who heard him were astounded at his understanding and his answers. When his parents saw him, they were astonished, and his mother said to him, "Son, why have you done this to us? Your father and I have been looking for you with great anxiety." And he said to them, "Why were you looking for me? Did you not know that I must be in my Father's house?" But they did not understand what he said to them. He went down with them and came to Nazareth, and was obedient to them; and his mother kept all these things in her heart. And Jesus advanced in wisdom and age and favor before God and man.

Action: The Temple dominated the city skyline. It was a place of constant activity as pilgrims came and went, sacrifices were offered, and prayers were being said. Rather than being intimidated by it all, Jesus feels completely at home here. Picture the scene with the teachers. Mary never had to search for Jesus before; she always knew right where he was. But now she and Joseph are themselves like the Magi, the shepherds, or like so many Christians who realize that they have somehow lost connection with God and are struggling to reconnect. What do Mary and Joseph feel as they realize that Jesus is gone and search for him? What do they feel when they find him serenely seated in the Temple?

Acknowledge: Read the passage a second time. Place yourself in the scene. Focus on the part that speaks to you. What thoughts, feelings, and desires are rising in your heart?

Relate: Speak to God what is in your heart. Perhaps sit with the boy Jesus in the Temple and share with him what you notice or what you are feeling. Or maybe you feel drawn to converse with Mary or Joseph. However you feel moved, be open and honest.

Receive: Read the passage one more time. Mary has pondered the Christmas events in her heart for many years. Ponder these events yourself and listen to what the Holy Spirit wants to reveal to you in today's prayer. Just receive for a few minutes.

Respond: You too are God's child, and the Temple is your Father's house. Savor the light of the Holy Spirit shining on your heart and respond to whatever God is giving you. Sit serenely with the Lord of the Temple for a few minutes before moving on.

SUGGESTIONS FOR JOURNALING

1. What struck me the most in today's reading was …
2. My strongest thought, feeling, or desire was …
3. I ended prayer wanting …
4. I saw Christmas in a new way …
5. I see my own family life from a new perspective …

After you've journaled, close with a brief conversation with God giving thanks for your prayer experience. Then pray an Our Father.

December 30 — Monday
Sixth Day in the Octave of Christmas

Preparation: *Come, Holy Spirit, enlighten the eyes of my heart.* Be present to the God who is always present to you. Call to mind his loving care for you and spend the first minute of your prayer just resting in the free, unearned gift of loving and being loved. Let gratitude rise in your heart.

Set the Scene: Ask God in your own words for a deeper sense of peace and joy in the birth of Jesus, that his light will shine in the dark corners of your heart and your world. The scene today is the same tremendous Temple and humble family but twelve years earlier. Jesus is forty days old and he is being presented in the Temple. Simeon has just taken the baby in his arms, blessed God, and prophesied over the baby and his mother (see Lk 2:22–35). Now a new person approaches, an elderly woman. Together, Simeon and Anna symbolize the longing for God in every human heart, and faithful Israel grown old awaiting its Savior. They also remind us of all the elderly who faithfully worship God and trust in his promises. Perhaps picture a faithful elderly woman you know who seems to always be at church. Read the passage through slowly and prayerfully.

LUKE 2:36–40 (LECTIONARY)

There was a prophetess, Anna, the daughter of Phanuel, of the tribe of Asher. She was advanced in years, having lived seven years with her husband after her marriage, and then as a widow until she was eighty-four. She never left the temple, but worshiped night and day with fasting and prayer. And coming forward at that very time, she gave thanks to God and spoke about the child to all who were awaiting the redemption of Jerusalem.

When they had fulfilled all the prescriptions of the law of the Lord, they returned to Galilee, to their own town of Nazareth. The child grew and became strong, filled with wisdom; and the favor of God was upon him.

Action: See Anna's face light up with joy as she recognizes the tiny Messiah. See that joy repeated every time she tells the story of this providential encounter. What is in her heart? What is in the hearts of her listeners who are awaiting the redemption of Jerusalem?

Acknowledge: Read the passage a second time. What is in your heart? What is it that you are awaiting? Has your face lit up with joy during this Christmas octave?

Relate: Speak to God what is in your heart. Picture God receiving you with the same joy with which Simeon and Anna received the Christ Child. If God had a refrigerator, your pictures and school drawings would be on it.

Receive: Read the passage a third time. Open your heart to receive what the Holy Spirit wants to reveal to you. If you are having a hard time receiving, gaze into the face of the Christ Child and let him look at you with love. What is in his heart for you?

Respond: God wants you to grow strong and be filled with his wisdom, for his favor or upon you. Receive whatever God wants to give you and let it help you to grow stronger in relationship with him. Savor his loving care for a few minutes before moving on.

SUGGESTIONS FOR JOURNALING
1. What spoke to me the most was …
2. I found myself wanting …
3. The strongest image or experience of God's love was …
4. I ended prayer wanting …
5. Anna shared the Good News with others. Who am I called to share this Good News with?

After you've journaled, close by giving thanks to God for your prayer time today, and then end with an Our Father.

December 31 — Tuesday
Seventh Day in the Octave of Christmas

Preparation: *Come, Holy Spirit, enlighten the eyes of my heart.* Be present to the God who is always present to you. Call to mind his loving care for you and spend the first minute of your prayer just resting in the free, unearned gift of loving and being loved. Let gratitude rise in your heart.

Lectio: Ask God in your own words for a deeper sense of peace and joy in the birth of Jesus, that his light will shine in the dark corners of your heart and your world. Speaking of light shining in the darkness, there is no Scripture passage that speaks of this more eloquently than the prologue of the Gospel according to Saint John. As you read this passage, picture him as an old man. The other apostles have all been martyred for their faith in Jesus, including his brother James, who died many years ago. He is surrounded by young believers who did not personally know Jesus. He wants them to know how much the birth of Jesus not only changed has own life, but even the course of human history. Read the passage slowly and prayerfully.

JOHN 1:1–18 (LECTIONARY)

In the beginning was the Word, and the Word was with God, and the Word was God. He was in the beginning with God. All things came to be through him, and without him nothing came to be. What came to be through him was life, and this life was the light of the human race; the light shines in the darkness, and the darkness has not overcome it.

A man named John was sent from God. He came for testimony, to testify to the light, so that all might believe through him. He was not the light, but came to testify to the light. The true light, which enlightens everyone, was coming into the world.

He was in the world, and the world came to be through him, but the world did not know him. He came to what was his own, but his own people did not accept him.

But to those who did accept him he gave power to become children of God, to those who believe in his name, who were born not by natural generation nor by human choice nor by a man's decision but of God.

And the Word became flesh and made his dwelling among us, and we saw his glory, the glory as of the Father's only-begotten Son, full of grace and truth.

John testified to him and cried out, saying, "This was he of whom I said, 'The one who is coming after me ranks ahead of me because he existed before me.'" From his fullness we have all received, grace in place of grace, because while the law was given through Moses, grace and truth came through Jesus Christ. No one has ever seen God. The only-begotten Son, God, who is at the Father's side, has revealed him.

Meditatio: Picture the millions of Christmas trees in homes, public squares and even shopping malls being lights in the darkness right now. Whether people realize it or not, they all symbolize Jesus, the Light of the World. You have experienced the light of Jesus enlightening your heart during this Advent pilgrimage. What has it felt like to be enlightened by Christ? Has his light helped you to see more clearly that you, too, are a beloved child of God? Reflect on their year's *Oriens* pilgrimage and where you have come since the First Sunday of Advent.

Oratio: Read the passage a second time. Notice the word, phrase, or idea that stands out to you personally. The Word who became flesh continues to dwell with you today. Share with him whatever has come up in your heart.

Contemplatio: Read the passage a third time, or just the part that speaks to you most strongly. Receive whatever is in God's heart for you. "From his fullness we have all received, grace in place of grace." Receive from his fullness, then rest in his loving care for a few minutes before moving on.

SUGGESTIONS FOR JOURNALING

1. I saw the light of Christ shining at Christmas when ...
2. The darkness feels most heavy and oppressive when ...
3. I received a new sense of being a child of God from ...
4. From his fullness I have received ...
5. How can I testify to the true light, which enlightens everyone?

After you've journaled, close by giving thanks to God for the light that was shining in your prayer time today, and then end with an Our Father.

January 1 — Wednesday
Eighth Day in the Octave of Christmas

THE BLESSED VIRGIN MARY, THE MOTHER OF GOD

Preparation: *Come, Holy Spirit, enlighten the eyes of my heart.* Be present to the God who is always present to you. Call to mind his loving care for you and spend the first minute of your prayer just resting in the free, unearned gift of loving and being loved. Let gratitude rise in your heart.

Lectio: Ask God in your own words for a deeper sense of peace and joy in the birth of Jesus, that his light will shine in the dark corners of your heart and your world. Read through the passage slowly and prayerfully.

NUMBERS 6:22–27 (LECTIONARY)

The LORD said to Moses: "Speak to Aaron and his sons and tell them: This is how you shall bless the Israelites. Say to them: The LORD bless you and keep you! The LORD let his face shine upon you, and be gracious to you! The LORD look upon you kindly and give you peace! So shall they invoke my name upon the Israelites, and I will bless them."

Meditatio: Aaron, Moses' older brother, became the high priest at the time of the exodus from Egypt. This ministry was continued by his sons. They are able to bless the people in God's name. Perhaps use the fruits of your meditation on Simeon to picture the "shining face" and "kindly look" with which God desires to look upon his people. How does it feel to know that God's face is shining as he looks upon you?

Oratio: Read the passage a second time. Speak to God what is on your heart. As a new year begins, in what way do you most desire to experience God's blessings? How did you experience God's blessings in 2024? Reflect on this question, then talk to the Lord about it. Thank him for the blessings of the previous year. Speak to him about the desires in your heart for the coming year. Picture him looking upon you kindly as you speak to him.

Contemplatio: Read the passage a third time. This time just receive what God wants to give you. What is in his heart for you? How has he blessed you, and will continue to bless you? What does his blessing stir up in your heart? Be with the God who loves you, and desires to give you every good thing, for a little while before moving on.

SUGGESTIONS FOR JOURNALING:
1. In the past year, I felt most blessed by …
2. The blessing I most desire to receive is …
3. My biggest obstacle to receive God's blessing could be …
4. This new year, I am worried that …
5. I am excited for …
6. God most desires to give me …

After you've journaled, close with a brief conversation with God giving thanks for your prayer experience. Then entrust your new year to the Mother of God by praying a Hail Mary.

January 2 — Thursday
Thursday before Epiphany

Preparation: *Come, Holy Spirit, enlighten the eyes of my heart.* Be present to the God who is always present to you. Call to mind his loving care for you and spend the first minute of your prayer just resting in the free, unearned gift of loving and being loved. Let gratitude rise in your heart.

Lectio: Ask God in your own words for a deeper sense of peace and joy in the birth of Jesus, that his light will shine in the dark corners of your heart and your world. The Book of Psalms is the Bible's hymn book, so we are today meditating on some song lyrics. Read through the passage slowly and prayerfully.

PSALM 98:1–6 (LECTIONARY)

Sing to the LORD a new song,
  for he has done wondrous deeds;
His right hand has won victory for him,
  his holy arm.
The LORD has made his salvation known:
  in the sight of the nations he has revealed his justice.
He has remembered his kindness and his faithfulness
  toward the house of Israel.
All the ends of the earth have seen
  the salvation by our God.
Sing joyfully to the LORD, all you lands;
  break into song; sing praise.
Sing praise to the LORD with the harp,
  with the harp and melodious song.
With trumpets and the sound of the horn
  sing joyfully before the King, the LORD. (Highlighted
text from NABRE)

Meditatio: "All the ends of the earth have seen the saving power of God." Perhaps an exaggeration at the time King David first set these words to music, but prophetically, Christmas is celebrated in every land, and

Christians are found on every continent. What are the wondrous deeds, such as unexpected answers to prayer, healings, conversions, or new life, that you have personally experienced? Reflect on these "everyday miracles."

Oratio: Read the passage a second time. The psalmist believes that his audience is God himself, that he is performing before the very throne of God. Wherever your prayer time is happening today, God is gazing at you with love from his throne. Speak to him from your heart. Know that he loves to hear your voice.

Contemplatio: Read the passage a third time. This time receive whatever is in God's heart for you — his thoughts, feelings, or desires. The Lord has remembered his kindness and faithfulness toward you, too. Rest in his loving compassion for a few minutes before moving on.

SUGGESTIONS FOR JOURNALING

1. I have witnessed God's wondrous deeds …
2. My strongest thought, feeling or desire was …
3. I received a new insight …
4. God wanted me to know …
5. If you were to sing to the Lord a new song, what would you sing?

After you've journaled, close with a brief conversation with God giving thanks for your prayer experience. Then pray an Our Father.

Friday before Epiphany

THE HOLY NAME OF JESUS

Mary and Joseph were both instructed by angels to name their child, "Jesus" (Mt 1:21; Lk 1:31). It was pronounced *Y'shua* in his native Aramaic and *IHΣOYΣ* (YE-SOUS) in the Greek language of the New Testament. This is "the name/ that is above every name, / that at the name of Jesus / every knee should bend, / of those in heaven and on earth and under the earth" (Phil 2:9b–10). St. Bernardine of Siena preached on the Holy Name of Jesus using the monogram IHS (transliterated from the first three letters of Jesus's name in Greek) and added the name of Jesus to the Hail Mary. This feast was added to the universal calendar in 1721, dropped in the reform after Vatican II, and re-added by Pope St. John Paul II.

Preparation: *Come, Holy Spirit, enlighten the eyes of my heart.* Be present to the God who is always present to you. Call to mind his loving care for you and spend the first minute of your prayer just resting in the free, unearned gift of loving and being loved. Let gratitude rise in your heart.

Lectio: Ask God in your own words for a deeper sense of peace and joy in the birth of Jesus, that his light will shine in the dark corners of your heart and your world. Today's passage is full of deep, rich ideas. Read slowly and savor it. Notice what speaks to your heart.

1 JOHN 2:29–3:6 (LECTIONARY)

If you consider that God is righteous, you also know that everyone who acts in righteousness is begotten by him.

See what love the Father has bestowed on us that we may be called the children of God. Yet so we are. The reason the world does not know us is that it did not know him. Beloved, we are God's children now; what we shall be has not yet been revealed. We do know that when it is revealed we shall be like him, for we shall see him as he is. Everyone who has this hope based on him makes himself pure, as he is pure.

Everyone who commits sin commits lawlessness, for sin is lawlessness. You know that he was revealed to take away sins, and in him there is no sin. No one who remains in him sins; no one who sins has seen him or known him.

Meditatio: Imagine for a moment being a poor orphan who was adopted by a rich and powerful man. This man had only one natural son, but he wanted to share his riches with other children. Having been adopted into the rich family, you would be expected to live in a manner worthy of your new family. The natural son would be your example for how to act. In a similar way, we have been adopted into God's family. God is good, and we are called to be good like God. When have you failed to live up to this noble calling? How can you draw strength to love from the one who is Love itself?

Oratio: Read the passage a second time. When God adopts us, he is not trying to make us into something new. Rather, he is restoring our birthright. You were created "in the beginning" to be God's beloved children. Through the envy of the Devil, we fell from grace and became convinced that we were not worthy of the Name of Jesus. But that is not true. God sent his Son to restore us to our original dignity. He then gave us the same Spirit that descended on Jesus and remains in him. It is the Spirit dwelling in you that enables you to live a righteous, pure, and holy life — the life you were created for! What desires arise in your heart? What fears or doubts? Bring them all to God; you can be completely honest with him. He already knows it all, he's just waiting for you to admit it.

Contemplatio: Read the passage a third time. How does God respond to your thoughts, feelings, and desires? How does he reassure you? Can you receive what God wants to give you? Receive God's love and abide in that love for a few minutes before moving on. Savor the love of the one in whose Name you have been saved and sealed for eternal life.

SUGGESTIONS FOR JOURNALING

1. What does it say to me that I am called a child of God?
2. What does it mean to be "like him, for we shall see him as he is"?
3. My strongest thought, feeling, or desire was ...
4. I have a hard time believing that ...
5. I need the Spirit to help me ...
6. God is calling me to ...

After you've journaled, close with a brief conversation thanking God for your adoption and for your time in prayer today. Then say the Name of Jesus nine times, slowly and prayerfully, as a closing prayer.

January 4 — Saturday
Saturday before Epiphany

REVIEW

Preparation: *Come, Holy Spirit, enlighten the eyes of my heart.* Call to mind God's loving care for you and spend the first minute of your prayer just resting in the free, unearned gift of loving and being loved. Let gratitude rise in your heart.

Grace of the Day: What is the desire of your heart? Try to notice what you must deeply desire. Then share it with God in your own words, being confident that he loves you and wants to give you every blessing.

Week in Review: Flip back through your past week's journal entries. As you do, notice what emerged in the conversation. Here are some questions to help you:

1. Where did I notice God, and what was he doing or saying?
2. How did I respond to what God was doing?
3. I really struggled with …
4. Prayer really seemed to click when …
5. I'm grateful for …
6. Now at the beginning of 2025, I most strongly want this new year to be a time of …
7. What one image of God's loving presence sticks with me most strongly?

Conclude by conversing with God about your week. **Acknowledge** what you have been experiencing. **Relate** it to him. **Receive** what he wants to give you. **Respond** to him. Then savor that image of God's loving presence and rest there for a minute or two. Close with an Our Father.

Week Six

Week Six

Well Begun Is Half Done

I learned a lot about prayer through writing this book. When I made my thirty-day retreat, I was introduced to the words of Saint Ignatius. He told retreatants to begin each prayer time by "Pausing for the space of an Our Father and considering how God Our Lord looks upon us." That line never really made sense to me, and it didn't make sense to people I later directed on retreat. I had an epiphany one day when watching an episode of *Tidying Up* with Marie Kondo on Netflix. Before she declutters a house, she pauses to thank the house and the things that it contains. OK, that's a little strange, but I noticed what she was doing. She wants people to begin their decluttering from a place of gratitude, and not from a place of frustration or feeling overwhelmed by all their stuff or fear that they will fail at decluttering.

Gratitude! That's what Ignatius was getting at. When we realize what God has done for us, how he has loved us faithfully and sent his Son to die for us, we cannot help but feel grateful. Gratitude is the antidote to anger, the antithesis of a consumer mentality, and the right attitude of a disciple. Our prayer should begin with gratitude.

God never stops loving us; the sun will stop shining before God stops loving you. But we don't always feel his love. As I begin prayer today, I might not feel particularly loved, blessed, or cared for by God. But God and I have a history together; I have experienced his loving care in the past, and I am sure to experience it again in the future. So, I begin my prayer by remembering a time that I felt particularly loved, blessed, and cared for. This helps me enter back into that moment and begin my prayer from a place of gratitude. Every Saturday I encourage you to sift your experiences and let one particular experience of love and closeness with God rise to the surface. I want you to save that experience and use it in the following days as a starting point for subsequent prayer times.

Saint Ignatius also encourages us to pray a "colloquy," which is a final conversation at the end of our prayer. This is a second opportunity for gratitude. Every prayer should begin and end with gratitude. Mother Church has the same idea when we traditionally pray both a grace before meals and a grace after meals. Our meals, however meager they may be, begin and end with gratitude.

The Church's Morning Prayer is called "Morning Praises" (*laudes*) to begin our day with gratitude. Prayer time at the end of the day is a chance to ask God for mercy (which is why we pray the Act of Contrition before bedtime) and then end the day with gratitude. The word *Eucharist* means "thanksgiving," as we begin and end our week with gratitude. Every Saturday, I write down my greatest blessing(s) of that week and put the slip of paper in a jar. At the end of the year, I dump out the jar and remember how God has blessed me. That way I can end one year and begin the next from a place of gratitude.

Congratulations on sticking with this book so far! You are past the halfway point. Know that God has so much more that he wants to give you. Don't believe me? Keep walking and find out.

Grace of the Week: This week we get to celebrate the Epiphany twice, once on Sunday and again on January 6. As you recognize the Christ Child as the King of Kings, pray for the grace of a deepening sense of your identity as a beloved child of God.

January 5 — Sunday
The Epiphany of the Lord (Observed)

The word *epiphany* means "manifestation." Jesus is manifest as more than just the King of the Jews, but as the King of all the nations. The traditional date of the Epiphany is January 6, but in the United States it is celebrated on the Sunday between January 2 and January 8. It is sometimes called "Little Christmas" and marks the arrival of the Wise Men (Magi) to the manger in Bethlehem. Saint Matthew saw ancient prophecies being fulfilled by the visit of the Magi, who represented the pagan nations. What birthday gift do we have to give to the newborn King of Kings?

Preparation: *Come, Holy Spirit, enlighten the eyes of my heart.* Be present to the God who is always present to you. Call to mind his loving care for you and spend the first minute of your prayer just resting in the free, unearned gift of loving and being loved. Let gratitude rise in your heart.

Set the Scene: Ask God in your own words for the grace of a deepening sense of your identity as a beloved child of our heavenly Father. Read through this passage slowly and prayerfully. Spend some time really setting the scene. What is the city like? What do the Magi look like? Picture the camels threading their way through the streets of Jerusalem, then Bethlehem. What does the house look like where the mother and child are?

MATTHEW 2:1–12 (LECTIONARY)

When Jesus was born in Bethlehem of Judea, in the days of King Herod, behold, magi from the east arrived in Jerusalem, saying, "Where is the newborn king of the Jews? We saw his star at its rising and have come to do him homage." When King Herod heard this, he was greatly troubled, and all Jerusalem with him. Assembling all the chief priests and the scribes of the people, he inquired of them where the Christ was to be born. They said to him, "In Bethlehem of Judea, for thus it has been written through the prophet: And you, Bethlehem, land of Judah, are by no means least among the rulers of Judah; since from you shall come a ruler, who is to shepherd my people Israel." Then Herod called the magi secretly and ascertained from them the time of the star's appearance. He sent them to Bethlehem and said, "Go and search diligently for the child. When you have found him, bring me word, that I too may go and do him homage." After their audience with the king they set out. And behold, the star that they had seen at its rising preceded them, until it came and stopped over the place where the child was. They were overjoyed at seeing the star, and on entering the house they saw the child with Mary his mother. They prostrated themselves and did him homage. Then they opened their treasures and offered him gifts of gold, frankincense, and myrrh. And having been warned in a dream not to return to Herod, they departed for their country by another way.

Action: The Magi have been on pilgrimage for a long time. Imagine what the journey from the East would have been like. Did they experience frustration? How did they encourage each other? What goes through their minds and hearts as they finally arrive? They find the child with his mother. Picture the relationship between mother and child.

Acknowledge: Read the passage a second time. You, too, have been on a pilgrimage. What thoughts, feelings, and desires are rising in your heart?

Relate: Share your thoughts and feelings with Mary, the Mother of God. How does she respond to you?

Receive: Read the passage a third time. What does the mother want to tell you about her Son? What does she want to tell you about yourself? What is in Mary's heart for you?

Respond: You have a gift to give. Open your treasures and respond by giving the Christ Child your gift.

SUGGESTIONS FOR JOURNALING

1. This time I was most drawn to …
2. I was particularly moved by …
3. The gift I want to give Jesus is …
4. I have been encouraged on this journey by …
5. Who have I encouraged on their pilgrimage of faith?

After you've journaled, close with a brief conversation with God about your prayer experience. Then pray an Our Father.

+

Bless your home today, or plan ahead for a blessing party on January 6. Instructions follow on the next page.

Blessing of the Home and Household on Epiphany

The chalking of the doors is a centuries-old practice throughout the world. While less known in the United States, it is becoming more celebrated and an easy tradition to adopt, dedicating our year to God, asking His blessing on our homes and on all who live, work, or visit us there. It can be encouraged for families to bring chalk for a general blessing after Mass of the Epiphany to bring home and mark their doors using the following prayer.

The leader should be the head of the household (the father, if the father is present). A reader may also be chosen. If one lives alone, the responses are also done by the leader himself, or one might invite friends and neighbors for the celebration. If the home has put out a Christmas crèche, that might be the best place to gather. The letters C, M, and B stand for the traditional names of the "Three Wise Men."

The leader makes the Sign of the Cross:

"+ In the Name of the Father, and of the Son, and of the Holy Spirit."
All reply, "Amen."

The leader greets those present in the following words: Let us praise God, who fills our hearts and homes with peace. Blessed be God forever.

Response: Blessed be God forever.

Leader: The Word became flesh and made his dwelling place among us. It is Christ who enlightens our hearts and homes with his love. May all who enter this home find Christ's light and love.

Reader: Listen to the words of the holy Gospel according to Matthew.

> When Jesus was born in Bethlehem of Judea, in the days of King Herod, behold, magi from the east arrived in Jerusalem, saying, "Where is the newborn king of the Jews? We saw his star at its rising and have come to do him homage." When King Herod heard this, he was greatly troubled, and all Jerusalem with him. Assembling all the chief priests and the scribes of the people, he inquired of them where the Christ was to be born. They said to him, "In Bethlehem of Judea, for thus it has been written through the prophet:
>
> > And you, Bethlehem, land of Judah, are by no means least among the rulers of Judah; since from you shall come a ruler, who is to shepherd my people Israel."
>
> Then Herod called the magi secretly and ascertained from them the time of the star's appearance. He sent them to Bethlehem and said, "Go and search diligently for the child. When you have found him, bring me word, that I too may go and do him homage." After their audience with the king they set out. And behold, the star that they had seen at its rising preceded them, until it came and stopped over the place where the child was. They were overjoyed at seeing the star, and on entering the house they saw the child with Mary his mother. They prostrated themselves and did him homage. Then they opened their treasures and offered him gifts of gold, frankincense, and myrrh.

And having been warned in a dream not to return to Herod, they departed for their country by another way.

The intercessions are then said:

Leader: The Son of God made his home among us. With thanks and praise let us call upon him.
Response: Stay with us, Lord.

Reader: Lord Jesus Christ, with Mary and Joseph you formed the Holy Family: remain in our home, that we may know you as our guest and honor you as our Head. We pray:
Response: Stay with us, Lord.

Reader: Lord Jesus Christ, you had no place to lay your head, but in the spirit of poverty accepted the hospitality of your friends: grant that through our help the homeless may obtain proper housing. We pray:
Response: Stay with us, Lord.

Reader: Lord Jesus Christ, the three kings presented their gifts to you in praise and adoration: grant that those living in this house may use their talents and abilities to your greater glory. We pray:
Response: Stay with us, Lord.

The leader then prays the blessing:

Lord God of heaven and earth, you revealed your only-begotten Son to every nation by the guidance of a star. Bless this house and all who inhabit it. Fill us with the light of Christ, that our concern for others may reflect your love. We ask this through Christ Our Lord.
Response: Amen.

The leader concludes the rite by signing himself or herself with the Sign of the Cross and saying: May Christ Jesus dwell with us, + keep us from all harm, and make us one in mind and heart, now and forever.
Response: Amen.

The leader takes the blessed chalk and marks the lintel (the doorframe above the door) on the inside of the main entrance to the house as follows: 20 + C + M + B + 25 (insert the last two digits of the current year).

Other doors may be chalked, for example, the bedroom doors by those who sleep in each room. It is preferable to end the celebration with a suitable song, for example, "O Come, All Ye Faithful" or "We Three Kings." Afterwards the family or host and invited guests might share a meal or a Twelfth Night party, or enjoy a king cake.

— Adapted from "Blessing of the Home and Household on Epiphany," USCCB, https://www.usccb.org/prayers/blessing-home-and-household-epiphany

January 6 — Monday
The Epiphany of the Lord (Traditional)

Preparation: *Come, Holy Spirit, enlighten the eyes of my heart.* Be present to the God who is always present to you. Call to mind his loving care for you and spend the first minute of your prayer just resting in the free, unearned gift of loving and being loved. Let gratitude rise in your heart.

Set the scene: Ask God in your own words for the grace of a deepening sense of your identity as a beloved child of God. The liturgical feast of the Epiphany is transferred to Sunday, but there's no reason why we can't also celebrate on its proper day. I love this first reading from the feast of the Epiphany. I've chosen imaginative prayer for this passage, but you could also use *lectio divina* if you would prefer. Isaiah is writing to a poor nation of exiles in a foreign land. Picture the dark clouds covering the nations (a reminder of the ninth plague in Egypt, recounted in Exodus 10:21–29). God's light is shining on his holy people, and they reflect that light to all the nations. Read through the passage slowly to set the scene.

ISAIAH 60:1–6 (LECTIONARY)

Rise up in splendor, Jerusalem! Your light has come, the glory of the Lord shines upon you. See, darkness covers the earth, and thick clouds cover the peoples; but upon you the LORD shines, and over you appears his glory. Nations shall walk by your light, and kings by your shining radiance. Raise your eyes and look about; they all gather and come to you: your sons come from afar, and your daughters in the arms of their nurses.

Then you shall be radiant at what you see, your heart shall throb and overflow, for the riches of the sea shall be emptied out before you, the wealth of nations shall be brought to you. Caravans of camels shall fill you, dromedaries from Midian and Ephah; all from Sheba shall

*come bearing gold and frankincense, and proclaiming
the praises of the LORD.*

Action: Use your imagination to picture the radiant faces of the returning exiles with hearts overflowing. The nations are bringing their wealth
as an act of thanksgiving, grateful that God's people have taught them
how to live in his glory, his truth, and his love. What is going on in the
hearts of God's Chosen People as the nations are coming to them?

Acknowledge: Read the passage a second time. What thoughts, feelings,
and desires are rising in your heart? Do you realize the precious gift you
have been given in knowing the one, true God?

Relate: Share your thoughts, feelings, and desires with God. Above all, let
gratitude rise in your heart.

Receive: Read the passage a third time. This time just receive what is in
God's heart for you. Savor the loving care that you have experienced from
him on this Christmas pilgrimage.

Respond: You are meant to be a light. Bask in God's light, receive his love
for you, and respond to what he wants to give you. Just be with him for a
minute or two before moving on.

SUGGESTIONS FOR JOURNALING
1. I felt thick clouds and darkness when …
2. It seemed like God's light was shining on me, and my heart
   overflowed, when …
3. This Christmas, God gave me the gift of …
4. I ended prayer wanting …
5. God is calling me to be more of a light to the world by …

After you've journaled, close with a brief conversation with God giving thanks for any "epiphanies" that you had in today's prayer experience. Then pray an Our Father.

Tuesday after Epiphany

ST. ANDRÉ BESSETTE

The eighth of twelve children born to Isaac and Clothilde, Alfred (his baptismal name) grew up in poverty in a small town in Quebec. His father died in a lumber accident when he was nine and his mother died three years later of tuberculosis. He also suffered from poor health and struggled to hold down a job. Noticing his prayerfulness and devotion, the pastor of his local parish presented him to the Congregation of the Holy Cross with a note to the superior, "I'm sending you a saint." They didn't want "saints" in poor health; the congregation only accepted him after the archbishop of Montreal intervened on his behalf. He took the name André (French for Andrew, perhaps a nod to his parish priest, who also bore this name). He cared for the sick and would rub them with oil taken from the Saint Joseph lamp in the congregation's college. So many recovered from illness that he developed a reputation for miraculous cures. He refused to take any credit, insisting that Saint Joseph was the source of the miracles. He was instrumental in the building of a basilica known as Saint Joseph's Oratory. He died on January 6, 1937, and is honored on this day in his home country of Canada.

Preparation: *Come, Holy Spirit, enlighten the eyes of my heart.* Be present to the God who is always present to you. Call to mind his loving care for you and spend the first minute of your prayer just resting in the free, unearned gift of loving and being loved. Let gratitude rise in your heart.

Lectio: Ask God in your own words for the grace of a deepening sense of your identity as a beloved child of God, and the gift to share that love with others. Today's passage is very short, but very rich. Read it slowly and savor it. Notice what speaks to your heart.

1 JOHN 4:7–10 (LECTIONARY)

Beloved, let us love one another, because love is of God;

everyone who loves is begotten by God and knows God. Whoever is without love does not know God, for God is love. In this way the love of God was revealed to us: God sent his only-begotten Son into the world so that we might have life through him. In this is love: not that we have loved God, but that he loved us and sent his Son as expiation for our sins.

Meditatio: We were made in the image and likeness of God. Since God is love, we too were made to love and be loved. When we love one another, we live up to our nature. Yet even though we have failed to love, God has loved us so much that he sent Jesus to die for our sins and restore us as adopted children of God. When have you failed to live up to this noble calling? How can you draw strength to love from the one who is Love itself?

Oratio: Read the passage a second time. Since God is love, every experience of true love is an experience of God. When have I experienced true love? How has that love shaped me, challenged me, called me, healed me? What desires arise in your heart? What fears or doubts? Bring them all to God; you can be completely honest with him.

Contemplatio: Read the passage a third time. How does God respond to what you have shared? What does he want to give you? Give God permission to love you. Receive God's love and abide in that love for a few minutes before moving on. Savor the time you have with the one who loves you so unconditionally that he sent his Son as expiation for your sins.

SUGGESTIONS FOR JOURNALING
1. When have I experienced the unconditional love of God?
2. How did I respond to that love?
3. I feel most fully alive when …
4. I need God to help me …
5. I ended prayer wanting …

After you've journaled, close with a brief conversation thanking God for the experience of knowing God a little more in your prayer time today. Then pray an Our Father.

January 8 — Wednesday
Wednesday after Epiphany

Preparation: *Come, Holy Spirit, enlighten the eyes of my heart.* Be present to the God who is always present to you. Call to mind his loving care for you and spend the first minute of your prayer just resting in the free, unearned gift of loving and being loved. Let gratitude rise in your heart.

Lectio: Ask God in our own words for the grace of a deepening sense of your identity as a beloved child of God, and the gift to share that love with others. You may have struggled with accepting God's love for you in yesterday's reading. That's a much more normal response than you may realize. The enemy never stops reminding us of our faults and failures. We humans have a tendency to rely on ourselves, which leads us to fall into sin. The more disappointed we are with ourselves, the more we assume that God must be disappointed too. Yet when we actually take time to draw close to God, we realize that he is rich in mercy. God deeply desires to pick us up, hug us, wash the filth away, and welcome us home. He has placed the Spirit within you so that you might accomplish his good and holy will. The Holy Spirit will help you receive the Father's love more deeply in today's prayer time.

1 JOHN 4:11–18 (LECTIONARY)

Beloved, if God so loved us, we also must love one another. No one has ever seen God. Yet, if we love one another, God remains in us, and his love is brought to perfection in us.

This is how we know that we remain in him and he in us, that he has given us of his Spirit. Moreover, we have seen and testify that the Father sent his Son as savior of the world. Whoever acknowledges that Jesus is the Son of God, God remains in him and he in God. We have come to know and to believe in the love God has for us.

God is love, and whoever remains in love remains in God and God in him. In this is love brought to perfection among us, that we have confidence on the day of judgment because as he is, so are we in this world. There is no fear in love, but perfect love drives out fear because fear has to do with punishment, and so one who fears is not yet perfect in love.

Meditatio: God didn't just give us the Spirit to make us feel warm and fuzzy. He gave us the Spirit because he knows that our own efforts will never be enough to respond to his love. The Spirit allows us to love God in return and to love one another as God has loved us. To the degree that we rely on the Spirit, we will find that the commandment of love is not burdensome. On the other hand, if we rely on our own efforts, we will find the commandment of love completely impossible to fulfill. But more than just action, God also wants union. He wants to remain with you and within you. If God's Spirit is in you, you have nothing to fear. Have you come to know and to believe in the love God has for you? Notice what word or phrase speaks to you most strongly.

Oratio: Read the passage a second time. Notice the thoughts, feelings, and desires that rise in your heart. Do you welcome God's love for you? Do you find yourself doubting? Do you need to ask for help in trying to love a particularly difficult person or situation — or yourself? Talk to God about whatever is coming up.

Contemplatio: Read the passage a third time. Receive what is in God's heart for you. Welcome his loving care for you and his desire to bring his love to perfection in you. Remain with God, and focus on God remaining in you, for a few minutes.

SUGGESTIONS FOR JOURNALING

1. Have I "come to know and to believe in the love God has" for me?
2. What is the biggest obstacle to remaining in his love?
3. The Spirit who moved over the waters is blowing in my life, creating in me …
4. I need help to …

5. I ended prayer wanting …
6. God seems to be asking of me …

After you've journaled, close with a brief conversation thanking God for your prayer experience. Then pray an Our Father.

January 9 — Thursday
Thursday after Epiphany

Preparation: *Come, Holy Spirit, enlighten the eyes of my heart.* Be present to the God who is always present to you. Call to mind his loving care for you and spend the first minute of your prayer just resting in the free, unearned gift of loving and being loved. Let gratitude rise in your heart.

Lectio: Ask God in our own words for the grace of a deepening sense of your identity as a beloved child of God, and the gift to share that love with others. We were made in the *image and likeness of God* (see Gn 1:26), and "*God is love*" (1 Jn 4:8). That means that we only achieve our true purpose as human beings when we learn to love others as God has loved us. Read the Scripture passage slowly and prayerfully.

1 JOHN 4:19—5:4 (LECTIONARY)

Beloved, we love God because he first loved us. If any-one says, "I love God," but hates his brother, he is a liar; for whoever does not love a brother whom he has seen cannot love God whom he has not seen. This is the commandment we have from him: Whoever loves God must also love his brother.

Everyone who believes that Jesus is the Christ is be-gotten by God, and everyone who loves the Father loves also the one begotten by him. In this way we know that we love the children of God when we love God and obey his commandments. For the love of God is this, that we keep his commandments. And his commandments are not bur-densome, for whoever is begotten by God conquers the world. And the victory that conquers the world is our faith.

Meditatio: The world can often feel like a cold, dark place — especially for those of us experiencing January in places like the upper Midwest of the United States. We sometimes wonder why God doesn't share more of his light and love with the world. The problem is not with God himself, but with all of us whose hearts have grown cold and dark. We were meant to add to the warmth and light around us, like candles lit with divine love. Name some people you know who are truly living up to their purpose of being God's image and likeness in the world. How do they inspire you to do the same.

Oratio: Read the passage again. "We love because he first loved us." We are not truly responsible to love as God loves until we have experienced God's love for us. Have you had such an experience this Christmas season? Talk to God about it. Share your thoughts, feelings, and desires with the one who loves you more than can be put into words.

Contemplatio: Read the passage a third time, or just the part that speaks to you most profoundly. Receive whatever God wants to give you. He is never done loving us, and he always has more that he wants to give us. Receive the more that God wants to give you today. Then rest in his loving care for a few minutes before moving on.

SUGGESTIONS FOR JOURNALING

1. Can I name anyone who most clearly lives the human vocation to love others like God loves us?
2. How have I experienced God's loving care for me recently?
3. Do I see the connection between keeping the commandments and living in love?
4. Who do I find most difficult to love?
5. In what area of my life is God inviting me to greater love?

After you've journaled, close with a brief conversation thanking God for your prayer experience. Then pray an Our Father.

January 10 — Friday
Friday after Epiphany

Preparation: *Come, Holy Spirit, enlighten the eyes of my heart.* Be present to the God who is always present to you. Call to mind his loving care for you and spend the first minute of your prayer just resting in the free, unearned gift of loving and being loved. Let gratitude rise in your heart.

Lectio: Ask God in our own words for the grace of a deepening sense of your identity as a beloved child of God, and the gift to share that love with others. The world around us is full of conflicting messages. People rise to fame seemingly overnight, and then post something stupid on social media and get canceled even quicker. We sometimes think of God's love as just as fickle. If I no longer feel loved in this moment, I can easily conclude that God has stopped loving me for some reason. God's love for us does not change from moment to moment, but our love can. Are we not likely to speak up about Jesus when our "church friends" are around, and to be quiet about our faith when surrounded by people who are hostile to faith? This is not how God loves us, and it shouldn't be how we love God. Read the Scripture passage slowly and prayerfully.

1 JOHN 5:5–13 (LECTIONARY)

Beloved: Who indeed is the victor over the world but the one who believes that Jesus is the Son of God?

This is the one who came through water and Blood, Jesus Christ, not by water alone, but by water and Blood. The Spirit is the one who testifies, and the Spirit is truth. So there are three who testify, the Spirit, the water, and the Blood, and the three are of one accord. If we accept human testimony, the testimony of God is surely greater. Now the testimony of God is this, that he has testified on behalf of his Son. Whoever believes in the Son of God has this testimony within himself. Whoever does not believe God has made him a liar by not believing the testimony God has given about his Son. And this is the testimony:

> *God gave us eternal life, and this life is in his Son. Who-*
> *ever possesses the Son has life; whoever does not possess*
> *the Son of God does not have life.*
>
> *I write these things to you so that you may know that*
> *you have eternal life, you who believe in the name of the*
> *Son of God.*

Meditatio: Knowing whom to trust, and whom to distrust, can keep us from falling to scammers. Saint John reminds us that we can trust Jesus, and trusting him will enable us to participate in his victory over the world. Jesus won this victory by his baptism into his true identity (the "water") and by being faithful to that identity even to death on the cross (the "blood"). It was through the Spirit that he received his true identity and remained in it. What does the Holy Spirit want to say to you about your true identity?

Oratio: Read the passage again. The Spirit himself comes to live within us. He guides us to truly live the Catholic Faith. Our deeds, in turn, witness to the truth that Jesus is risen. They speak to the truth that Jesus himself is eternal life, and having Jesus means that we can fear nothing, not even death. What part of this passage speaks to you, personally? Talk to God about the thoughts, feelings, and desires that are rising within you. Or the fears, worries, and concerns that you might have. The Spirit will help you be honest with God.

Contemplatio: Read the passage a third time, or just the part that speaks to you most profoundly. Receive whatever God wants to give you. The one who breathed life into Adam's nostrils wants to continue to give you life today. Receive whatever he gives, then be with the Lord for a few minutes before moving on.

SUGGESTIONS FOR JOURNALING
1. What does it mean to have God's testimony within oneself?
2. I heard or received the testimony that …
3. I struggle with the fear that …
4. I sensed the Holy Spirit moving me to …

5. I feel a new confidence that …

After you've journaled, close with a brief conversation thanking God for your prayer experience. Then pray an Our Father.

January 11 — Saturday
Saturday after Epiphany

REVIEW

Preparation: *Come, Holy Spirit, enlighten the eyes of my heart.* Call to mind God's loving care for you and spend the first minute of your prayer just resting in the free, unearned gift of loving and being loved. Let gratitude rise in your heart.

Grace of the Day: What is the desire of your heart? Try to notice what you must deeply desire. Then share it with God in your own words, being confident that he loves you and wants to give you every blessing.

Week in Review: Flip back through your past week's journal entries. As you do, notice what emerged in the conversation. Here are some questions to help you:

1. Where did I notice God, and what was he doing or saying?
2. How did I respond to what God was doing?
3. I found myself struggling with …
4. I'm grateful for …
5. Living my identity as a child of God means …
6. I feel called to a new way of believing, living, or loving …
7. This past week, my strongest sense, image, moment, or experience of God's loving presence was …

Conclude by conversing with God about your week. **Acknowledge** what you have been experiencing. **Relate** it to him. **Receive** what he wants to give you. **Respond** to him. Then savor that image of God's loving presence and rest there for a minute or two. Close with an Our Father.

Week Seven

Christmas Ends Today. Long Live Christmas!

The liturgical season of Christmas officially ends today, on the feast of the Baptism of the Lord. But for many people, Christmas ended two weeks ago. You probably have neighbors who threw out their trees on Christmas Day. Christmas music disappears from the radio, and all the Christmas specials are over. Many families try to keep the holiday spirit through the New Year's celebration, but then it's back to work again. Christmas seems to slowly fade into Ordinary Time. When the Baptism of the Lord rolls around, it's more like the Church catching up with the world than a proper celebration of the end of Christmas. Christmas needs a better ending.

It seems that our ancestors found a way to make Christmas last for forty days. In medieval and Tudor England, homes would be decorated with greenery such as laurel, holly, ivy, and rosemary at Christmas time. There was no rush to take it down; it was left decorating the house until Candlemas Eve. Candlemas is the old English name for the feast of the Presentation, celebrated on February 2. This was the day that Jesus was presented in the Temple (see Lk 2:22–40). The Mass for the day welcomes the Christ Child with a blessing of candles and a procession into church.

I have come to really appreciate February 2 as a kind of "last hurrah" of Christmas. If you waited and didn't light your tree until Christmas, you get the benefit of enjoying it for forty days (or until the needles fall off, whichever comes first). I think that we need a little more Christmas cheer to carry us through the post-holiday blues and the cold days of January. Even though the liturgical season of Christmas is over, your own personal celebration can continue. I encourage you to keep your Advent wreath and Nativity crèche up in the spirit of the old English tradition. Keep praying and keep savoring the light of Christ shining from the manger scene. God has more to give. Let us keep our hearts open to receive.

Grace of the Week: This week we will return to Ordinary Time. Our readings this week are drawn from the Letter to the Hebrews. Ask for the grace to see how greatly God has exulted our Emanuel, who humbled himself for our salvation.

+

The U.S. bishops' "9 Days for Life" novena begins soon. Learn more at www.9daysforlife.com.

January 12 — Sunday
Baptism of the Lord

Preparation: *Come, Holy Spirit, enlighten the eyes of my heart.* Be present to the God who is always present to you. Call to mind his loving care for you and spend the first minute of your prayer just resting in the free, unearned gift of loving and being loved. Let gratitude rise in your heart.

Set the Scene: Ask God in your own words that he might reveal to you the unsurpassable glory of our humble Emmanuel. Read the passage through, slowly and prayerfully. It is the fifteenth year of the reign of Tiberius Caesar and the Spirit of God has called John the Baptist into the desert. He preaches repentance to prepare the people for the Messiah. Read the passage and set the scene in your mind. Picture the wilderness and the great throng of people coming to repentance. Picture their yearning for a Savior.

LUKE 3:15–16, 21–22 (LECTIONARY)

The people were filled with expectation, and all were asking in their hearts whether John might be the Christ. John answered them all, saying, "I am baptizing you with water, but one mightier than I is coming. I am not worthy to loosen the thongs of his sandals. He will baptize you with the Holy Spirit and fire."

After all the people had been baptized and Jesus also had been baptized and was praying, heaven was opened and the Holy Spirit descended upon him in bodily form like a dove. And a voice came from heaven, "You are my beloved Son; with you I am well pleased."

Action: Jesus, who will baptize "with the Holy Spirit and fire," is first baptized in the Spirit. How does John the Baptist feel as he watches his prophecy come true before his very eyes? How does Jesus feel when he hears the voice from heaven? How does God the Father feel watching his Son receiving baptism?

Acknowledge: Read the passage a second time. What do you feel, or what is it that you personally long for, as you hear John proclaiming, "One mightier than I"? Do you desire to be baptized with the Holy Spirit and fire (perhaps a reference to Pentecost)? Are you fearful, doubtful, or eager?

Relate: Jesus himself is praying and has a powerful experience of the Father's love for him. Imagine him now seated a little distance away contemplating what just happened. Sit with Jesus by the Jordan River. Share with him what is on your heart.

Receive: Read the passage a third time. How does Jesus respond to you? Remember, you too were once baptized. What does Jesus want to teach you about your baptism? Be open to whatever God is offering — a word, thought, or feeling, a new understanding or insight.

Respond: How does this moment, and your own baptism, look different when seen through Jesus's eyes? Continue the conversation for a little while. Then just rest in the love God has for you, the same love that the Father has for his only-begotten Son.

SUGGESTIONS FOR JOURNALING

1. The part of this Scripture passage that most spoke to me was …
2. I sensed that God was with me and wanted me to know …
3. I was hesitant/afraid that/excited by …
4. I ended prayer wanting …
5. I now see my own baptism in a new way …

After you've journaled, close with a brief conversation giving thanks to God, Father, Son, and Spirit, for your prayer experience. Then pray an Our Father.

Monday of the First Week in Ordinary Time

SAINT HILARY, BISHOP AND DOCTOR OF THE CHURCH

Hilary was born in AD 315 in Poitiers, in what is now France. He grew up as a pagan but converted to Christianity through the reading of Scripture. He became the bishop of his hometown at a time when Christianity was under threat from the heresy known as Arianism. Hilary refused the emperor's order to sign a condemnation of the bishop Athanasius, and was banished to Phrygia (present-day Turkey). He continued writing and defending the Trinity and the divinity of Christ until his opponents decided that he would cause them less trouble if they sent him back to France. Hilary was welcomed by his people. He died in 368.

Preparation: *Come, Holy Spirit, enlighten the eyes of my heart.* Be present to the God who is always present to you. Call to mind his loving care for you and spend the first minute of your prayer just resting in the free, unearned gift of loving and being loved. Let gratitude rise in your heart.

Lectio: Ask God in your own words that he might reveal to you the unsurpassable glory of our humble Emanuel. We will spend this week with selections from the Letter to the Hebrews, which are used as the first readings for the daily Masses in the first week of Ordinary Time. This book of the Bible is often included among the letters of Saint Paul, though it says nothing about who wrote it nor to whom it was written. It makes an extended argument that Jesus is the true High Priest of the new and eternal covenant, which replaces the covenant that God made with the Israelites on Mount Sinai. Because we have a perfect priest, we can have confidence in receiving forgiveness of sins and a path into heaven. His example also teaches us how we should live as Christians. Earthly kings and princes have power, honor, and glory. How much more so are the awesome powers of the one who not only commands angels, but also had a hand in creating them? Read the passage slowly and prayerfully.

HEBREWS 1:1–6 (LECTIONARY)

Brothers and sisters: In times past, God spoke in partial and various ways to our ancestors through the prophets; in these last days, he spoke to us through the Son, whom he made heir of all things and through whom he created the universe,

who is the refulgence of his glory,
    the very imprint of his being,
and who sustains all things by his mighty word.
When he had accomplished purification from sins,
he took his seat at the right hand of the Majesty on high,
as far superior to the angels
as the name he has inherited is more excellent than theirs.
For to which of the angels did God ever say:
You are my son; this day I have begotten you?
Or again:
I will be a father to him, and he shall be a Son to me?
And again, when he leads the first-born into the world, he says:
Let all the angels of God worship him.

Meditatio: You might use your imagination to picture Jesus seated on a mighty throne next to God his Father, surrounded with the glory of a million sunrises, and being attended by as many mighty angels. The angels are bowing down in worship and singing hymns of praise. The Father gazes at his Son with the same look as at his baptism yesterday: "You are my beloved son; with you I am well pleased."

Oratio: Read the passage a second time. Jesus is looking at you with the same mixture of love and pride as his Father looks at him (Jn 15:9).

Though seated on a lofty throne, Jesus is not full of himself, but desiring to share with you the abundance that he has received. What do you desire? Talk to Jesus out loud or in your heart. You can be completely honest. He already knows what is in your heart, but he has been patiently waiting for you to say something.

Contemplatio: Read the passage a third time. This time, receive whatever is in Jesus's heart for you. Then spend a few minutes in gratitude that he chooses to be friends with you and cherishes your friendship.

SUGGESTIONS FOR JOURNALING
1. I saw Jesus in a new light …
2. I never realized before …
3. I shared with Jesus that …
4. Jesus wanted me to know …
5. I ended prayer grateful for …

After you've journaled, close with a brief conversation giving thanks to God for the glory of your prayer experience. Then pray an Our Father.

January 14 — Tuesday
Tuesday of the First Week in Ordinary Time

Preparation: *Come, Holy Spirit, enlighten the eyes of my heart.* Be present to the God who is always present to you. Call to mind his loving care for you and spend the first minute of your prayer just resting in the free, unearned gift of loving and being loved. Let gratitude rise in your heart.

Lectio: Ask God in your own words that he might reveal to you the unsurpassable glory of our humble Emmanuel. Yesterday we met Jesus in power and glory. Today we reflect on the fact that Jesus's kingship is not honored here and now. In fact, when the King of Kings entered our world, he was rejected by men and died a humiliating death on the cross. As you read this passage, picture Jesus hanging on the cross with dignity and grace, and calmly telling the good thief hanging next to him, "Amen, I say to you, today you will be with me in Paradise" (Lk 23:43).

HEBREWS 2:5–12 (LECTIONARY)

It was not to angels that God subjected the world to come, of which we are speaking. Instead, someone has testified somewhere:

> *What is man that you are mindful of him,*
> *or the son of man that you care for him?*
> *You made him for a little while lower than the angels;*
> *you crowned him with glory and honor,*
> *subjecting all things under his feet.*

In "subjecting" all things to him, he left nothing not "subject to him." Yet at present we do not see "all things subject to him," but we do see Jesus "crowned with glory and honor" because he suffered death, he who "for a little while" was made "lower than the angels," that by the grace of God he might taste death for everyone.

For it was fitting that he, for whom and through whom all things exist, in bringing many children to glory, should make the leader to their salvation perfect through suffering. He who consecrates and those who are being consecrated all have one origin. Therefore, he is not ashamed to call them "brothers" saying:

I will proclaim your name to my brethren,
in the midst of the assembly I will praise you.

Meditatio: Do you find yourself sometimes doubting that Jesus is the King of Kings and that all power in heaven and on earth has been given to him? Do you sometimes wonder if the Christian life is truly worth living? Would we be silent if the crowds around us were shouting to crucify Our Lord and friend? Jesus is not ashamed to be our brother; are we ashamed to admit to family and friends that we follow him?

Oratio: Read the passage a second time. The one who was "crowned with glory and honor" stands humbly before you in this place of prayer. Turn to him. Thank him that he is not ashamed to be your brother, and not afraid to taste death for you and for everyone. Speak to him whatever is on your heart.

Contemplatio: Read the passage a third time. Receive whatever is in Jesus's heart for you. Though he is higher than the angels and all things are subject to him, he cherishes your friendship. Though you may have given up on him a thousand times, he has not given up on you. Rest in his loving care for you for a little while before moving on.

SUGGESTIONS FOR JOURNALING
1. God feels distant when …
2. I have been burdened by …
3. I sensed Jesus that was encouraging me with a reminder that …
4. I ended prayer strengthened by …

5. My prayer today gave me a new insight into how I should think, respond, or act …

_____

_____

_____

_____

_____

_____

_____

_____

_____

_____

_____

_____

_____

After you've journaled, close with a brief conversation thanking Jesus for being your Savior and for meeting you in your prayer time today. Then pray an Our Father.

January 15 — Wednesday
Wednesday of the First Week in Ordinary Time

Preparation: *Come, Holy Spirit, enlighten the eyes of my heart.* Be present to the God who is always present to you. Call to mind his loving care for you and spend the first minute of your prayer just resting in the free, unearned gift of loving and being loved. Let gratitude rise in your heart.

Lectio: Ask God in your own words that he might reveal to you the unsurpassable glory of our humble Emmanuel. Today's passage is full of rich references to biblical stories. Let the images of death, fear, and slavery speak to you as you read this passage slowly and prayerfully.

HEBREWS 2:14–18 (LECTIONARY)
Since the children share in blood and Flesh, Jesus likewise shared in them, that through death he might destroy the one who has the power of death, that is, the Devil, and free those who through fear of death had been subject to slavery all their life. Surely he did not help angels but rather the descendants of Abraham; therefore, he had to become like his brothers and sisters in every way, that he might be a merciful and faithful high priest before God to expiate the sins of the people. Because he himself was tested through what he suffered, he is able to help those who are being tested.

Meditatio: Suffering is part of the human condition. Our greatest sufferings come not from the burden of daily life, but from fear of death and slavery to sin. Jesus wants to set us free, and so he assumes our human nature and suffers with us in order to set us free. How does Jesus's self-giving love undo the sin of Adam and Eve? What does his compassion say to you about your value?

Oratio: Read the passage a second time. "If you were the only person in the world, Jesus would still have suffered all that just for you." Are there ways you are being tested by what you are suffering? What does Jesus's suffering love stir in your heart? Talk to him about it.

Contemplatio: Read the passage a third time. This time, receive whatever is in Jesus's heart for you. Spend a few minutes with the God who suffers with you and suffers for you.

SUGGESTIONS FOR JOURNALING

1. I saw Jesus in a new light …
2. I never realized before …
3. I shared with Jesus that …
4. Jesus wanted me to know …
5. I ended prayer inspired to …

After you've journaled, close with a brief conversation giving thanks to God for your prayer experience. Then pray an Our Father.

January 16 — Thursday
Thursday of the First Week in Ordinary Time

Preparation: *Come, Holy Spirit, enlighten the eyes of my heart.* Be present to the God who is always present to you. Call to mind his loving care for you and spend the first minute of your prayer just resting in the free, unearned gift of loving and being loved. Let gratitude rise in your heart.

Lectio: Ask God in your own words for the grace to see Jesus as our High Priest and to see yourself as a participant in the priesthood of Jesus Christ. Half of today's Scripture is a quote from Psalm 95, which references Exodus 17:1–7. Though the Israelites have been freed from slavery by God's mighty hand and brought safely through the Red Sea, they begin to doubt God as soon as the water runs low. Read the passage slowly and prayerfully.

HEBREWS 3:7–14 (LECTIONARY)
The Holy Spirit says:

> Oh, that today you would hear his voice,
>> "Harden not your hearts as at the rebellion
>> in the day of testing in the desert,
> where your ancestors tested and tried me
>> and saw my works for forty years.
> Because of this I was provoked with that generation
>> and I said, 'They have always been of erring heart,
>> and they do not know my ways.'
> As I swore in my wrath,
>> 'They shall not enter into my rest.'"

Take care, brothers and sisters, that none of you may have an evil and unfaithful heart, so as to forsake the living God. Encourage yourselves daily while it is still "to-

day," so that none of you may grow hardened by the deceit of sin. We have become partners of Christ if only we
hold the beginning of the reality firm until the end.

Meditatio: How often have we experienced God's loving care for us, perhaps an answer to prayer or a situation that worked out better than we
could have hoped, only to face another crisis or challenge and immediately imagine the worst possible outcome? The "deceit of sin" can cause
us to have evil and unfaithful hearts. We can look back and see many ex-
amples of answered prayer, so why do we continue to look forward with
fear and trepidation? Reflect on the times you might have had an attitude
not unlike that of the Israelites.

Oratio: Read the passage a second time. Jesus trusted in his Father and
was not disappointed. Talk to him about your doubts and ask him how
he was able to have such trust.

Contemplatio: Read the passage a third time. This time, receive whatever
is in Jesus's heart for you. Receive whatever encouragement he offers you,
then spend a few minutes in quiet contemplation before moving on.

SUGGESTIONS FOR JOURNALING
1. I was guilty of "testing and trying God" when …
2. Jesus reminded me …
3. The biggest thing that makes me doubt God is …
4. I was encouraged by …
5. I ended prayer with a new way of thinking, seeing, or acting …

After you've journaled, close with a brief conversation giving thanks to God for his patience with you. Then pray an Our Father.

January 17 — Friday

Friday of the First Week in Ordinary Time

SAINT ANTHONY, ABBOT

Anthony was born in Egypt around AD 251. When he was about eighteen years old, he heard the Bible passage read in church, "Go, sell what you have, and give to [the] poor and you will have treasure in heaven; then come, follow me" (Mk 10:21). He believed this was a personal invitation from God directed to him. He gave away his earthly possessions and went out into the desert to live a simple life of prayer and penance. During this period, the Church transitioned from persecuted minority to a kind of state religion. Christianity became too easy and comfortable for the likes of many. Those who desired to give their all for Jesus went out into the desert and joined Anthony. He wrote a rule for them which became the foundation of the monastic life. What message does God have for you in today's Scripture passage?

Preparation: *Come, Holy Spirit, enlighten the eyes of my heart.* Be present to the God who is always present to you. Call to mind his loving care for you and spend the first minute of your prayer just resting in the free, unearned gift of loving and being loved. Let gratitude rise in your heart.

Lectio: Ask God in your own words that he might reveal to you the unsurpassable glory of our humble Emmanuel. After creating the world in six days, God rested on the seventh day (see Gn 2:3). His "rest" is used as a reference to the heavenly kingdom, where we too will find eternal rest for our labors. Will we be able to enter in? Read the passage below slowly and prayerfully.

HEBREWS 4:1–5, 11 (LECTIONARY)

Let us be on our guard while the promise of entering into his rest remains, that none of you seem to have failed. For in fact we have received the Good News just as our ances-

tors did. But the word that they heard did not profit them, for they were not united in faith with those who listened. For we who believed enter into that rest, just as he has said: As I swore in my wrath, "They shall not enter into my rest," and yet his works were accomplished at the foundation of the world. For he has spoken somewhere about the seventh day in this manner, And God rested on the seventh day from all his works; and again, in the previously mentioned place, They shall not enter into my rest.

Therefore, let us strive to enter into that rest, so that no one may fall after the same example of disobedience.

Meditatio: God desires all to come to know him and be saved (see 1 Tm 2:4). That means that God wants you to enter into his rest, and sent Jesus to open the way for you and remove the obstacles that keep you from entering in. In order to receive life, you have only to trust him and obey him. Are there obstacles that keep you from trusting your life to God?

Oratio: Read the passage a second time. Are there fears rising in your heart? Do you doubt him, or yourself? Be honest with God about what you are thinking and feeling. Remember, he sent his only Son to die for you, so great is his love for you.

Contemplatio: Read the passage a third time. This time, receive whatever is in God's heart for you. Then spend a few minutes entering into his "rest" here and now.

SUGGESTIONS FOR JOURNALING
1. "God's rest" means to me …
2. I saw salvation in a new light …
3. My heart was troubled by …
4. God wanted me to know …
5. Today's prayer time has inspired me …

After you've journaled, close with a brief conversation giving thanks to God for your prayer experience. Then pray an Our Father.

January 18 — Saturday
Saturday of the First Week in Ordinary Time

REVIEW

Preparation: *Come, Holy Spirit, enlighten the eyes of my heart.* Call to mind God's loving care for you and spend the first minute of your prayer just resting in the free, unearned gift of loving and being loved. Let gratitude rise in your heart.

Grace of the Day: What is the desire of your heart? Try to notice what you most deeply desire. Then share it with God in your own words, being confident that he loves you and wants to give you every blessing.

Week in Review: Flip back through your past week's journal entries. As you do, notice what emerged in the conversation. Here are some questions to help you:

1. Where did I notice God, and what was he doing or saying (in your prayer time or in your daily experiences)?
2. How did I respond to what God was doing?
3. I felt God's love most strongly when …
4. I found myself struggling with …
5. I'm grateful for …
6. This past week, my strongest sense, image, moment, or experience of God's loving presence was …

_____

_____

_____

_____

_____

_____

Conclude by conversing with God about your week. **Acknowledge** what you have been experiencing. **Relate** it to him. **Receive** what he wants to give you. **Respond** to him. Then savor that image of God's loving presence and rest there for a minute or two. Close with an Our Father.

Week Eight

Discernment of Spirits

"How do I know it's really God that is speaking to me?" St. Ignatius of Loyola was a master at the discernment of spirits. He distinguishes between the Spirit of God and the enemy. He says that if we are generally living for ourselves and engaging in mortal sin, the enemy spirit will try and keep us lulled into a false sense of security and comfort. For example, "Just a quick look at porn never hurt anyone." Or, "You can quit drinking tomorrow. Tonight, enjoy yourself." For this kind of person, the work of the Good Spirit will feel like a slap in the face or an alarm clock (some people use the phrase "spiritual two-by-four") because the Good Spirit has to shake us out of our stupor so that we can see the danger to our soul.

On the other hand, for a person who is generally growing in faith, living for God, and trying to avoid sin, the work of the two spirits is the opposite. The enemy wants us to stop growing, so he will propose imaginary obstacles, discouragements, distractions, and confusion. The voice of the enemy will be accusatory: "You're not good enough"; "You're broken"; "No one could love someone like you"; "You're doing it wrong; everyone else is having a better retreat than you"; "You missed a few days; you might as well quit and try again next year." These thoughts come with feelings of unrest, fear, and sometimes panic. The Good Spirit, on the other hand, will be encouraging and supportive and come with a sense of peace. The Good Spirit will remind us that we are loved, valued, and forgiven. Even when we need a "wake-up call," it will feel more like a gentle nudge.

Saint Ignatius also wants us to be aware of the pattern of consolation and desolation. For Ignatius, consolation is "when some interior movement in the soul is caused, through which the soul comes to be inflamed with love of its Creator and Lord; and when it can, in consequence, love no created thing on the face of the earth in itself, but in the Creator of them all." From this place of being close to God, we experience clarity and "every increase in hope, faith, and charity, and all interior joy which calls and attracts to heavenly things and to the salvation of one's soul, quieting it and giving it peace in its Creator and Lord."

Desolation, on the other hand, is, according to Ignatius, "the contrary of [the above], such as darkness of soul, disturbance in it, movement to things low and earthly, the unquiet of different agitations and temptations, moving to want of confidence, without hope, without love, when one finds oneself all lazy, tepid, sad, and as if separated from his Creator and Lord."

Desolation is when we hear the voice of the enemy more strongly; right seems wrong and bad choices come easily. Think of consolation like a sunny day and desolation like a dark and stormy night. In desolation we should not make a change, but we should keep walking on the road that we saw clearly when we were in consolation. In consolation we should draw strength from God's love and prepare ourselves for when desolation comes again.

This pattern of easy and difficult, comfort and struggle, is to be expected on pilgrimages. Some days we feel strong and comforted and we make progress easily. Other days are windy, cold, exhausting, and we find that we have to put our heads down and just focus on putting one blistered foot in front of the other. The difficult times test your mettle and force you to face your fears and burdens. The times of resistance are actually the times of the most spiritual growth. So do not be discouraged if you have faced resistance, difficulties praying each day, and lots of struggles from inside of you and from outside. Resistance is a sign that you are on the right road and that, by overcoming obstacles, spiritual progress is happening. The only way to have a "bad pilgrimage" is to quit. Just keep walking, however slowly it may be, and you will eventually reach your goal.

Grace of the Week: This week we will use Sunday's reading, the wedding feast at Cana, as our theme. We will delve into the scriptural idea that the love between a husband and wife reflects God's love for his people. Pray for the grace to more deeply appreciate the total gift of Christ the bridegroom to his bride, the Church.

January 19 — Sunday
Second Sunday in Ordinary Time

Preparation: *Come, Holy Spirit, enlighten the eyes of my heart.* Be present to the God who is always present to you. Call to mind his loving care for you and spend the first minute of your prayer just resting in the free, unearned gift of loving and being loved. Let gratitude rise in your heart.

Set the Scene: Ask God in you or own words for the grace to more deeply appreciate the total gift of Christ the Bridegroom to his Bride, the Church. Read the passage through and picture the scene in your mind. A Jewish wedding is always a big deal, no matter how poor the couple might be. The feast probably lasted several days. This poor couple didn't have enough wine to satisfy all their guests. Picture a courtyard or hall full of happy guests. What time of day is it? What time of year is it? What are people wearing?

JOHN 2:1–11 (LECTIONARY)

There was a wedding at Cana in Galilee, and the mother of Jesus was there. Jesus and his disciples were also invited to the wedding. When the wine ran short, the mother of Jesus said to him, "They have no wine." And Jesus said to her, "Woman, how does your concern affect me? My hour has not yet come." His mother said to the servers, "Do whatever he tells you." Now there were six stone water jars there for Jewish ceremonial washings, each holding twenty to thirty gallons. Jesus told them, "Fill the jars with water." So they filled them to the brim. Then he told them, "Draw some out now and take it to the headwaiter." So they took it. And when the headwaiter tasted the water that had become wine, without knowing where it came from — although the servers who had drawn the water knew — the headwaiter called the bridegroom and said to him, *"Everyone serves good wine first, and then when people have drunk freely, an inferior one; but you have kept the good wine until now."* Jesus did this as the beginning of his signs at Cana in Galilee and so revealed his glory, and his disciples began to believe in him.

Action: Notice the panic in the kitchen as the wine runs short. Picture Our Lady gently attentive to this human need. Then see the busy servers who have dropped everything to begin hauling, by hand, a very large amount of water out of a nearby well. What is going on in the hearts of the different participants, and in the heart of Jesus and of Mary? Place yourself in the scene.

Acknowledge: Read the passage a second time. Wine is often used in the Bible as a symbol for joy and gladness. When has the wine run short in your life? How did you respond to times that seemed hopeless and without joy? What is going on in your heart?

Relate: Turn to Jesus (or Mary) after the scene is over. Have a conversation with one or the other of them, or both. Where is the wine running short in your life, or in the lives of people you love? Share your thoughts, feelings, desires, fears.

Receive: Read the passage a third time. How does Jesus (or Mary) respond? What is Jesus telling you to do? Can you see Mary's loving care for you? Be open to whatever God wants to give you today.

Respond: What deeper truth do they want you to realize? After a little conversation, let yourself just enjoy their company for a little while.

SUGGESTIONS FOR JOURNALING
1. The wine ran short in my life when …
2. I felt Jesus (or Mary) saying to me …
3. I need to ask for …
4. The servers put a lot of work into drawing water without grumbling or complaining. Where am I called to work with-

out worrying about the results?
5. When was I surprised by joy?

After you've journaled, close with a brief conversation giving thanks to God for the new wine of your prayer experience. Then pray an Our Father.

January 20 — Monday

Monday of the Second Week in Ordinary Time

Preparation: *Come, Holy Spirit, enlighten the eyes of my heart.* Be present to the God who is always present to you. Call to mind his loving care for you and spend the first minute of your prayer just resting in the free, un-earned gift of loving and being loved. Let gratitude rise in your heart.

Set the Scene: Ask God for the grace to more deeply appreciate the total gift of Christ the Bridegroom to his Bride, the Church. Inspired by Sunday's passage, we will spend this week on the theme of bridegroom and bride. We begin, once again, in the beginning. Read the passage through and picture the scene in your mind. God has created a single man who is living the original "life in paradise." Despite having every creature comfort, his life is missing something that he can't quite name until God creates the final masterpiece of creation.

GENESIS 2:18–25

The LORD God said: It is not good for the man to be alone. I will make a helper suited to him. So the LORD God formed out of the ground all the wild animals and all the birds of the air, and he brought them to the man to see what he would call them; whatever the man called each living creature was then its name. The man gave names to all the tame animals, all the birds of the air, and all the wild animals; but none proved to be a helper suited to the man.

So the LORD God cast a deep sleep on the man, and while he was asleep, he took out one of his ribs and closed up its place with flesh. The LORD God then built the rib that he had taken from the man into a woman. When he brought her to the man, the man said:

"This one, at last, is bone of my bones

> *and flesh of my flesh;*
> *This one shall be called 'woman,'*
>   *for out of man this one has been taken."*
> *That is why a man leaves his father and mother*
> *and clings to his wife, and the two of them become*
> *one body.*
> *The man and his wife were both naked, yet they felt*
> *no shame.*

Action: Use your imagination to picture the scene. What is Adam thinking and feeling as the scene unfolds? Why does God allow him to live the single life for a while? What does it feel like to wake up and discover the most beautiful of all the creatures, and to realize that she was made for him as he was made for her?

Acknowledge: Read the passage a second time. Notice the thoughts, feelings, and desires that arise in your heart. God knows what you really want and what you were made for. But he wants to work with you to help you discover it.

Relate: Turn to God and share with him whatever is on your heart. Tell him what you long for and desire, or how it feels to have a partner who is "bone of my bones, and flesh of my flesh." What more do you still need or want? Speak to your Creator honestly.

Receive: Read the passage a third time. How does God respond to the desires of your heart? What deeper truth does he want to reveal to you? Be open to whatever he is giving you — a thought, word, or recognition of an even deeper desire.

Respond: God is with you. He wants you to be happy. Enjoy the time with the Lord who has been your helper and guide these many pilgrimage days. Savor his company for a few minutes before moving on.

SUGGESTIONS FOR JOURNALING
1. The part of today's reading that most stood out to me was …

2. My life seemed to be missing something when …
3. God desires to give me …
4. I find fulfillment when …
5. I ended prayers with a sense that …

_____

_____

_____

_____

_____

_____

_____

_____

_____

_____

_____

_____

_____

_____

_____

_____

After you've journaled, close with a conversation giving thanks to God for your prayer experience. Then pray an Our Father.

January 21 — Tuesday
Tuesday of the Second Week in Ordinary Time

SAINT AGNES, VIRGIN AND MARTYR

Tradition holds that Agnes was a young Roman noblewoman martyred under Emperor Diocletian around AD 304. She is one of seven women mentioned by name in the Roman Canon of the Mass (Eucharistic Prayer I). Her name comes from the Latin word *agnus*, meaning lamb. She is often depicted holding a lamb in witness to the innocence of her youth and her virginity. On this day in Rome, the Holy Father blesses the sheep whose wool will be woven into the pallia worn by archbishops.

Preparation: *Come, Holy Spirit, enlighten the eyes of my heart.* Be present to the God who is always present to you. Call to mind his loving care for you and spend the first minute of your prayer just resting in the free, un-earned gift of loving and being loved. Let gratitude rise in your heart.

Lectio: Ask God in your own words for the grace to more deeply appreciate the total gift of Christ the Bridegroom to his Bride, the Church. The Bible often compares God's covenant with Israel to the marriage covenant between a husband and a wife (see Is 5:1–7; 54:4–8; Jer 2–3; Ez 16 and 23). In this passage from Saint Paul, we hear that Christ himself is the Bridegroom and we, the Church, are his Bride. Saint Paul wants us to see Christ on the cross as a man giving himself completely for the one he loves. It might help to have a crucifix present as you pray today. Read this passage slowly and prayerfully.

EPHESIANS 5:25–32

Husbands, love your wives, even as Christ loved the church and handed himself over for her to sanctify her, cleansing her by the bath of water with the word, that he might present to himself the church in splendor, without spot or wrinkle or any such thing, that she might be holy and without

238 January 21 — Tuesday

blemish. So [also] husbands should love their wives as their own bodies. He who loves his wife loves himself. For no one hates his own flesh but rather nourishes and cherishes it, even as Christ does the church, because we are members of his body.

"For this reason a man shall leave [his] father and [his] mother
   and be joined to his wife,
and the two shall become one flesh."

This is a great mystery, but I speak in reference to Christ and the church.

Meditatio: Turn over in your mind the personal aspect of Jesus's sacrifice on the cross. The Lord of the Universe, who was worshiped by the Magi, loves me, was born for me, and allowed himself to be tortured to death to pay for my sins. In his eyes, I am worthy. Jesus nourishes and cherishes me. The problem with the Gospel message is not that it's too old-fashioned and boring; the problem with the Gospel message is that it's almost too good to be true. But it is true! What does it mean that Jesus loves me like a bridegroom loves his bride? Allow the truth of God's personal love for you to sink in.

Oratio: Read the passage a second time. Allow your thoughts, feelings, and desires to rise to the surface. It may be a little harder for men to picture this kind of love. Perhaps a man might imagine a fellow soldier who died to rescue him from the enemy. Is it hard for you to accept love? Have you been convinced that Jesus loves everyone but you? Speak to God what is in your heart.

Contemplatio: Read the passage a third time. Now receive what is in God's heart for you. What does he want to give you — a thought, feeling, or desire? Accept, receive, welcome his love. Give God permission to love you. Then spend a few minutes savoring his love before moving on.

SUGGESTIONS FOR JOURNALING

1. Among the ideas in today's prayer, I find it hardest to accept …
2. I want to believe that …
3. My soul feels at peace when …
4. I felt true love when …
5. I can best respond to God's love by …

After you've journaled, close by offering a few words of thanks to God for his love that you have experienced on your prayer journey. Then pray an Our Father.

Wednesday of the Second Week in Ordinary Time

DAY OF PRAYER FOR THE LEGAL PROTECTION OF UNBORN CHILDREN

In the United States of America, today shall be observed as a particular day of penance for violations to the dignity of the human person committed through acts of abortion, and of prayer for the full restoration of the legal guarantee to the right to life. Offer some fasting or another suitable penance today. Pray for a continual deepening conversion to the value of every life, and that the value of human life be reflected in our culture and our laws.

Preparation: *Come, Holy Spirit, enlighten the eyes of my heart.* Be present to the God who is always present to you. Call to mind his loving care for you and spend the first minute of your prayer just resting in the free, unearned gift of loving and being loved. Let gratitude rise in your heart.

Lectio: Ask God in your own words for the grace to more deeply appreciate the total gift of Christ the Bridegroom to his Bride, the Church. In today's passage, the Prophet Hosea accuses Israel of being an unfaithful wife, chasing other gods like a married woman chasing other lovers. And yet, despite her unfaithfulness, God remains faithful. Read the passage slowly and prayerfully.

HOSEA 2:14–20

I will lay waste her vines and fig trees,
of which she said, "These are the fees
my lovers have given me";
I will turn them into rank growth
and wild animals shall devour them.
I will punish her for the days of the Baals,

for whom she burnt incense,
When she decked herself out with her rings and her jewelry,
    and went after her lovers —
    but me she forgot — oracle of the LORD.
Therefore, I will allure her now;
    I will lead her into the wilderness
    and speak persuasively to her.
Then I will give her the vineyards she had,
    and the valley of Achor as a door of hope.
There she will respond as in the days of her youth,
    as on the day when she came up from the land of Egypt.
On that day — oracle of the LORD —
You shall call me "My husband,"
    and you shall never again call me "My baal."
I will remove from her mouth the names of the Baals;
    they shall no longer be mentioned by their name.
I will make a covenant for them on that day,
    with the wild animals,
With the birds of the air,
    and with the things that crawl on the ground.
Bow and sword and warfare
    I will destroy from the land,
    and I will give them rest in safety.

Meditatio: God always keeps his promises. He led Israel out of slavery in Egypt, protected them from their enemies, and sent them his Son. How would God feel when his Chosen People kept trying out other gods? The name *Baal* means "Lord" and referred to deities worshiped by the Canaanite peoples in the vicinity of Israel. There is a temptation to try out whichever God our neighbors are worshiping, or to turn away from God when he doesn't seem to give us what we need as quickly as we want it to happen. What things will cause me to skip Sunday Mass? Are they not, in that moment, more important to me than God? What else do I "worship" in hopes of receiving blessing?

Oratio: Read the passage a second time. Listen to your heart, a heart that longs for the love, joy, and peace that only Jesus can bring. Allow your thoughts, feelings, and desires to surface. Don't feel ashamed of your unfaithfulness. God knows your heart even better than you do. What do you need to let go of? What do you need to cling to? God hasn't given up on you! Trust that he has long been waiting for you to turn back to him.

Contemplatio: Read the passage a third time. Sometimes it can be hard to look at God and let him look at you. Recall for a moment his abundant blessings to you at Christmas time. How much he treasures you! Receive what God wants to give you, then rest in his loving care for a few minutes before moving on.

SUGGESTIONS FOR JOURNALING
1. I have experienced the faithfulness of God when ...
2. Sometimes I put this in front of God ...
3. I have felt God's love calling me to ...
4. I struggle to believe that ...
5. As I end my prayer time, I find myself wanting ...

After you've journaled, close with a conversation with God giving thanks for your prayer experience. Then pray an Our Father.

January 23 — Thursday
Thursday of the Second Week in Ordinary Time

Preparation: *Come, Holy Spirit, enlighten the eyes of my heart.* Be present to the God who is always present to you. Call to mind his loving care for you and spend the first minute of your prayer just resting in the free, unearned gift of loving and being loved. Let gratitude rise in your heart.

Lectio: Ask God in your own words for the grace to more deeply receive the total gift of Christ the Bridegroom to his Bride, the Church. We return to the Song of Songs, the book that we meditated on right at the beginning of our *Oriens* journey. Every love story, even Hallmark movies, contain some kind of crisis where it appears that the lovers will be lost to each other. This passage captures so beautifully the agony of the lover as she seeks her beloved. Connect, if you can, with the feelings in her heart. Read the passage slowly and prayerfully.

SONG OF SONGS 3:1–4
On my bed at night I sought him
*   whom my soul loves —*
I sought him but I did not find him.
"Let me rise then and go about the city,
*   through the streets and squares;*
Let me seek him whom my soul loves."
*   I sought him but I did not find him.*
The watchmen found me,
*   as they made their rounds in the city:*
*   "Him whom my soul loves — have you seen him?"*
Hardly had I left them
*   when I found him whom my soul loves.*
I held him and would not let him go
*   until I had brought him to my mother's house,*
*   to the chamber of her who conceived me.*

Meditatio: This passage is about more than a lovestruck maiden; it is about everyone who has lost a loved one. We can see in her agony the desperation of a parent who has lost a child, a man who just got dumped by the girl of her dreams, the lost feeling after burying a parent or losing a close friend to an untimely death. We can see the searching of Mary Magdalene for the Crucified Lord (see Jn 20:17). More than anything, two people who love each other long to be together. God loves you and he longs to be with you, as we heard yesterday. But we too long to be with God. Our deepest desire points us to the deep, unconditional love of God. He is the one for whom our hearts yearn and ache.

Oratio: What word or passage really speaks to you? Read the passage a second time. Then share with God what is on your heart — your thoughts, feelings, and desires. If you are noticing pain, anguish, or fear surface, don't stuff it back down. Speak to God honestly about it.

Contemplatio: Read the passage a third time. This time, open your heart to receive whatever God wants to share with you. Is there some new insight or understanding that emerges? Cling to him, hold him fast, and do not let him go today. Rest in his love for you for a few minutes before moving on.

SUGGESTIONS FOR JOURNALING

1. I most deeply desire ...
2. Thinking about God's love for me makes me afraid that ...
3. I really want to hear God say or to know in my heart ...
4. I feel most satisfied, joyful, and peaceful when ...
5. I ended prayer wanting ...

After you've journaled, close with a conversation with God giving thanks for your prayer experience. Then pray an Our Father.

Friday of the Second Week in Ordinary Time

ST. FRANCIS DE SALES

Born August 21, 1567, Francis was the son of a senator from the province of Savoy in France. His father sent him to study law to follow in his own footsteps. Francis, however, felt a call to become a priest. He patiently and gently won his father's consent. Part of his conversion happened when he heard a Calvinist preach on predestination and became convinced that he was predestined for eternal damnation. Eventually he came to experience God's love for him and realized that a loving God would not predestine anyone to hell. He was an effective preacher himself and converted many Calvinists back to the Catholic Faith. At the age of thirty-five, he was named bishop of Geneva, then being run as an autocratic theocracy by none other than John Calvin himself. He spent twenty years conquering his quick temper, so much so that he became famous for his gentle character. His many pamphlets on the Faith, famous books, and exhaustive correspondence made him a patron of the Catholic press.

Preparation: *Come, Holy Spirit, enlighten the eyes of my heart.* Be present to the God who is always present to you. Call to mind his loving care for you and spend the first minute of your prayer just resting in the free, unearned gift of loving and being loved.

Set the Scene: Ask God for the grace to more deeply appreciate the total gift of Christ the Bridegroom to his Bride, the Church. Today's passage comes from the last book in the Bible. The harlot is not a real person but rather a symbol of the anti-Church, a personification of all the forces of false worship within Israel and in the larger pagan world. She, and all who worship false gods, will be cast into hell. But those who have been faithful to God will be the bride of the Lamb, washed clean in his blood and clothed in righteous deeds. Allow the symbolic language to come alive for you.

REVELATION 19:1–9

After this I heard what sounded like the loud voice of a great multitude in heaven, saying:

> *"Alleluia!*
> *Salvation, glory, and might belong to our God,*
> *for true and just are his judgments.*
> *He has condemned the great harlot*
> *who corrupted the earth with her harlotry.*
> *He has avenged on her the blood of his servants."*

They said a second time:

> *"Alleluia! Smoke will rise from her forever and ever."*
> *The twenty-four elders and the four living creatures fell down and worshiped God who sat on the throne, saying, "Amen. Alleluia."*

A voice coming from the throne said:

> *"Praise our God, all you his servants,*
> *[and] you who revere him, small and great."*

Then I heard something like the sound of a great multitude or the sound of rushing water or mighty peals of thunder, as they said:

> *"Alleluia!*
> *The Lord has established his reign,*
> *[our] God, the almighty.*
> *Let us rejoice and be glad*
> *and give him glory.*
> *For the wedding day of the Lamb has come,*
> *his bride has made herself ready.*
> *She was allowed to wear*

a bright, clean linen garment."
(The linen represents the righteous deeds of the holy ones.)

Then the angel said to me, "Write this: Blessed are those who have been called to the wedding feast of the Lamb." And he said to me, "These words are true; they come from God."

Action: At the time these words were written, the Church of Christ was experiencing persecution from Jews and Gentiles alike. Saint John envisions that the Lamb who was slain will win the final victory over his enemies, and that his faithful followers will be vindicated. Where do you see yourself in the scene?

Acknowledge: Read the passage again. This time pay attention to your own thoughts and feelings. You have been called to the wedding feast of the Lamb. Have you accepted his invitation and readied yourself for the feast, or are you putting it off as more pressing matters take your attention? Have you allowed other things to take the place of the one true God in your life? Have you faced persecution because for your worship of the Lamb?

Relate: Turn to Jesus, the Lamb of God. He is humble and patient with you. Share with him what this passage has stirred up in your heart.

Receive: Read the passage a third time. Receive what is in his heart for you. Listen to his words or receive his love, even if it is just a word or a feeling of comfort. Remember that the Lamb is also the Good Shepherd, and you too are a beloved lamb.

Respond: Have a conversation with the Good Shepherd, then relax into his loving care for you for a few minutes before moving on.

SUGGESTIONS FOR JOURNALING
1. The image that really struck me was …
2. I found myself fearful of or disturbed by …

3. The Lamb wants to give me …
4. God is calling me to …
5. In what area of my life do I want to experience his power, his peace, his victory, and his love most powerfully?

_____

_____

_____

_____

_____

_____

_____

_____

_____

_____

_____

_____

_____

_____

_____

_____

After you've journaled, close with thanksgiving to God the Father and to the Lamb for your prayer experience. End with an Our Father.

January 25 — Saturday
The Conversion of Saint Paul, Apostle

How did it happen that Saul of Tarsus, zealous Jewish student of the law and persecutor of Christians, became Paul the apostle who would die for the Jesus he had once blasphemed? He was present when Stephen was martyred and consented to the stoning (see Acts 7:58; 8:1). Perhaps Stephen loved his enemies and prayed for those who persecuted him. Saint Paul went on to become a great missionary of the Gospel in pagan lands. He wrote many of the letters of the New Testament. The site of his burial is now one of the four major basilicas of the city of Rome. Saint Paul reminds us to never despair, for the love of God can conquer even the hardest of hearts. Let us open our hearts to God's love today.

REVIEW

Preparation: *Come, Holy Spirit, enlighten the eyes of my heart.* Call to mind God's loving care for you and spend the first minute of your prayer just resting in the free, unearned gift of loving and being loved. Let gratitude rise in your heart.

Grace of the Day: What is the desire of your heart? Try to notice what you must deeply desire. Then share it with God in your own words, being confident that he loves you and wants to give you every blessing.

Week in Review: Flip back through your past week's journal entries. As you do, notice what emerged in the conversation. Here are some questions to help you:

1. Where did I notice God, and what was he doing or saying?
2. How did I respond to what God was doing?
3. I felt God's love most strongly when …
4. I found myself struggling with …
5. I'm grateful for …
6. This past week, my strongest sense, image, moment, or expe-

rience of God's loving presence was …
7. How do I feel God calling me to stand against the powers of darkness and witness to the victory of the Lamb?

_____

_____

_____

_____

_____

_____

_____

_____

_____

_____

_____

_____

_____

_____

_____

_____

_____

_____

Conclude by conversing with God about your week. **Acknowledge** what you have been experiencing. **Relate** it to him. **Receive** what he wants to give you. **Respond** to him. Then savor that image of God's loving presence and rest there for a minute or two. Close with an Our Father.

Week Nine

Week Nine

Relational Prayer (ARRR)

I want to teach you a third prayer form, called Relational Prayer or "A-R-R-R." You've already seen this prayer form as part of Imaginative Prayer. Let's review the four steps: **Acknowledge** what is going on inside of you — your thoughts, feelings, and desires. **Relate**, or share with the Lord what is going on inside of you. **Receive** what God wants to give you. **Respond** to what the Lord just gave you.

This prayer form can stand on its own as a way of praying with the experiences of everyday life. Let's say that I'm on the phone with a relative who is upset that my family's plans for Christmas don't fit her expectations. She says that "Some people need to learn to be more flexible; they can't just expect the rest of the world to revolve around them." I get angry and say something like "Do you have any idea how difficult it is to get all of my family on the same page?" "I'm just saying," she says, "I hope you all have yourselves a nice Christmas." And that's the end of the conversation. (This episode is purely fictional.)

Great, now I've lost the Christmas spirit, and I'm going to be angry the rest of the day. "Does she have any idea how hard I work to make everyone happy and no one's ever happy …" I could stew on it, or I could let God help me. So I go sit in my prayer corner, or just focus on God wherever I happen to be. I start, as we always do, "*Come Holy Spirit, enlighten the eyes of my heart …*" I call to mind God's loving care for me that I experienced in a recent prayer time and let gratitude rise in my heart. I'm still feeling angry, but I know that I'm not alone.

Next, I **acknowledge** what is going on inside of me. Why am I angry? I notice the feelings that happened before I got angry, such as feeling unappreciated or disrespected or not valued. I might realize that I have a wound in this area that makes these kinds of conversations hurt more than they should.

Now I turn to Jesus and focus on him. I could also speak to God the Father, the Holy Spirit, or Mother Mary. It might help to call to mind a favorite image such as the Good Shepherd or Divine Mercy or one of the memorable moments when Jesus and I connected through Imaginative Prayer. I **relate** what's going and share my heart with him. The important

257

thing here is that my focus needs to shift from me and my problem to the Lord. First it was me looking at my problem, then both of us looking at my problem, and now I'm looking at him.

I **receive** what he wants to give me: a feeling, a thought, a reminder, a Scripture passage, and the like. I also might realize things like I tend to be a pleaser, or I was already frustrated before the conversation started.

I **respond** by acting out of this new vision and letting go of something, or by resolving to handle things differently next time with Jesus's help. I might need to pray for her or forgive her. I might need to forgive myself. I end with gratitude to God.

Try it for yourself at some point this week. You will be surprised how much this simple prayer form will change your life. Sharing your burdens with God makes them shrink like snow in the sunshine.

Grace of the Week: Our pilgrim journey ends next Sunday with the Feast of the Presentation. We will focus our attention on Scripture readings that talk about the worship of God and the Temple. We will ask for the grace to understand the meaning of the words "Temple of the Holy Spirit."

January 26 — Sunday
Third Sunday in Ordinary Time

Preparation: *Come, Holy Spirit, enlighten the eyes of my heart.* Be present to the God who is always present to you. Call to mind his loving care for you and spend the first minute of your prayer just resting in the free, unearned gift of loving and being loved. Let gratitude rise in your heart.

Set the Scene: Ask God in your own words for the grace to understand the meaning of the words "Temple of the Holy Spirit." Remember the week we spent following Jesus through the synagogues of Galilee, listening to him preach and watching him cast out demons and heal the sick? Jesus now returns to his hometown. They have heard about his miracles, and they are most likely very skeptical. "He never did anything special when he lived here. What are these reports we are hearing?" Read the passage and use your imagination to picture the Sabbath morning light shining through the synagogue windows and the candlelight reflecting off familiar faces as Jesus stands up to read from the scroll.

LUKE 1:1–4; 4:14–21 (LECTIONARY)

Since many have undertaken to compile a narrative of the events that have been fulfilled among us, just as those who were eyewitnesses from the beginning and ministers of the word have handed them down to us, I too have decided, after investigating everything accurately anew, to write it down in an orderly sequence for you, most excellent Theophilus, so that you may realize the certainty of the teachings you have received.

Jesus returned to Galilee in the power of the Spirit, and news of him spread throughout the whole region. He taught in their synagogues and was praised by all.

He came to Nazareth, where he had grown up, and went according to his custom into the synagogue on the sabbath day. He stood up to read and was handed a scroll of the prophet Isaiah. He unrolled the scroll and found the passage where it was written:

> The Spirit of the Lord is upon me,
> because he has anointed me
> to bring glad tidings to the poor.
> He has sent me to proclaim liberty to captives
> and recovery of sight to the blind,
> to let the oppressed go free,
> and to proclaim a year acceptable to the Lord.

Rolling up the scroll, he handed it back to the attendant and sat down, and the eyes of all in the synagogue looked intently at him. He said to them, "Today this Scripture passage is fulfilled in your hearing."

Action: The year acceptable to the Lord is a jubilee (see Lv 25:8–13), a whole year that was like a Sabbath. A familiar passage, but with an unexpected twist: Jesus is the fulfillment of these words; in him, the kingdom of God has come. Jesus has long wanted to tell everyone who he is and why he was born. But he has kept silent until now. What is in Jesus's heart as he stands up to read? What is going on in the hearts and minds of his listeners on this Sabbath morning?

Acknowledge: Read the passage a second time. If you have been raised in a Christian household, you have in some way "grown up" with Jesus. Perhaps we, like them, have not yet seen the whole Jesus. What is in your heart on this Sunday morning (or whenever you are reading)? What are you thinking, feeling, hoping for, expecting?

Relate: Sometimes we can be scandalized by Jesus. Just like the people of Nazareth, he seems to be speaking to others and healing others, but not to me. Where do you feel poor, or like a captive who needs to be liberated, a blind person who longs to see, or someone oppressed by a heavy burden? Does Jesus seem to care? Speak to God what is on your heart.

Receive: Read the passage a third time. Today, Jesus reads these words to you. Today, this Scripture is fulfilled in your hearing. What does Jesus want to tell you or give you right now? Can you open your heart to receive?

Respond: Now respond to whatever Jesus has given you. If he doesn't seem to be giving you anything, tell him how that feels. He will spend all day with you, if you are open to it. Spend a few minutes just resting in the jubilee moment of a God who loves you and has come to meet you.

SUGGESTIONS FOR JOURNALING

1. How did the Holy Spirit communicate God's presence to me?
2. It can be hard to see my own blind spots. How did my expectations blind me when I began my *Oriens* pilgrimage?
3. God has offered me … (freedom, hope, a new way of seeing, rest, a specific gift)
4. How do I now see Jesus differently?
5. What does Jesus see when he looks at me?
6. I end prayer with a deeper desire for …

After you've journaled, close with a brief conversation giving thanks to God for his Anointed One present in your prayer experience. Then pray an Our Father.

January 27 — Monday
Monday of the Third Week in Ordinary Time

Preparation: *Come, Holy Spirit, enlighten the eyes of my heart.* Be present to the God who is always present to you. Call to mind his loving care for you and spend the first minute of your prayer just resting in the free, unearned gift of loving and being loved. Let gratitude rise in your heart.

Set the Scene: Ask God in your own words to understand what it means to be a "Temple of the Holy Spirit." Noah spent years building the ark in order to save himself, his family, and all the animals from destruction. Finally the waters have receded and the earth is dry. What is the first thing that the Bible records them building? Read the passage below and picture the scene in your mind.

GENESIS 8:15–22

Then God said to Noah: Go out of the ark, together with your wife and your sons and your sons' wives. Bring out with you every living thing that is with you — all creatures, be they birds or animals or crawling things that crawl on the earth — and let them abound on the earth, and be fertile and multiply on it. So Noah came out, together with his sons and his wife and his sons' wives; and all the animals, all the birds, and all the crawling creatures that crawl on the earth went out of the ark by families.

Then Noah built an altar to the LORD, and choosing from every clean animal and every clean bird, he offered burnt offerings on the altar. When the LORD smelled the sweet odor, the LORD said to himself: Never again will I curse the ground because of human beings, since the desires of the human heart are evil from youth; nor will I ever again strike down every living being, as I have done.

All the days of the earth,
seedtime and harvest,
cold and heat,
Summer and winter,
and day and night
shall not cease.

Action: Most of us would not think to immediately build an altar and sacrifice some of the animals that just survived the flood (don't worry — he brought seven pairs of the clean animals, so he had some to spare). Sacrificing animals to the gods was a common practice in the ancient world. Most cultures explained that the gods were somehow fed by these sacrifices and therefore it would appease their wrath and make them well-disposed toward tiny humans. The Bible presents Noah's sacrifice as an act of thanksgiving. It also keeps man and God in proper relationship. By giving some of the animals back to God, man is paying tribute to the true owner of all that is.

Acknowledge: Read the passage a second time. What does this passage stir up inside of you? How has God rescued you "from the flood"? How might you be called to acknowledge God as the true owner of all that is?

Relate: The God of Noah is with you now. Speak to him from your heart.

Receive: Read the passage a third time. How does God respond to what you have shared with him? Receive his loving care for you.

Respond: God no longer requires animal sacrifices because Jesus has offered the one perfect sacrifice. He is looking for a contrite and loving heart. Open your heart to him, and rest in his loving care for you for a few minutes before moving on.

SUGGESTIONS FOR JOURNALING
1. Today I learned that …
2. What did this passage stir up in me today?
3. In what ways can I join my offerings to the one perfect sac-

rifice that Jesus offered on the cross?
4. God is pleased with …
5. God wants to promise me that …

After you've journaled, close with a brief conversation giving thanks to God for whatever blessings you received today. Then pray an Our Father.

Tuesday of the Third Week in Ordinary Time

ST. THOMAS AQUINAS, DOCTOR OF THE CHURCH

Born in 1225 to minor nobility, Thomas's family intended for him to become abbot of the prestigious monastery of Monte Cassino in southern Italy. He was sent to the University of Naples for his theology studies. It was there that he encountered the Dominicans, a new mendicant order that preached the Gospel, lived in poverty, and begged for their food. Against his family's objections, Thomas left the Benedictines to become a Dominican. His classmates, seeing that he was big and quiet, assumed that he was quite stupid, and gave him the nickname "The Dumb Ox." In reality, Thomas was thinking too hard to say much. Once he started teaching and writing, he became known as one of the greatest philosophers and theologians of all time.

Preparation: *Come, Holy Spirit, enlighten the eyes of my heart.* Be present to the God who is always present to you. Call to mind his loving care for you and spend the first minute of your prayer just resting in the free, unearned gift of loving and being loved. Let gratitude rise in your heart.

Set the Scene: Ask God in your own words for the grace to understand how you are a "Temple of the Holy Spirit." Moses has led the people out of slavery in Egypt. In Exodus chapter 24, Moses ratifies the covenant between God and the Israelites. He then remains in the cloud on the top of Mount Sinai for forty days and forty nights. During that time, God dictates six chapters of instructions to Moses on how to build the Tabernacle, how to consecrate the priests and ordain them, and the kinds of sacrifices that they will be offering. Our reading below is a brief excerpt from these instructions. Use your imagination to picture what is being described.

EXODUS 25:1–9, 26, 31–37

The LORD spoke to Moses: Speak to the Israelites: Let them receive contributions for me. From each you shall receive the contribution that their hearts prompt them to give me. These are the contributions you shall accept from them: gold, silver, and bronze; violet, purple, and scarlet yarn; fine linen and goat hair; rams' skins dyed red, and tahash skins; acacia wood; oil for the light; spices for the anointing oil and for the fragrant incense; onyx stones and other gems for mounting on the ephod and the breastpiece. They are to make a sanctuary for me, that I may dwell in their midst. According to all that I show you regarding the pattern of the tabernacle and the pattern of its furnishings, so you are to make it.

You shall also make four rings of gold for it and fasten them at the four corners, one at each leg.

You shall make a menorah of pure beaten gold — its shaft and branches — with its cups and knobs and petals springing directly from it. Six branches are to extend from its sides, three branches on one side, and three on the other. On one branch there are to be three cups, shaped like almond blossoms, each with its knob and petals; on the opposite branch there are to be three cups, shaped like almond blossoms, each with its knob and petals; and so for the six branches that extend from the menorah. On the menorah there are to be four cups, shaped like almond blossoms, with their knobs and petals. The six branches that go out from the menorah are to have a knob under each pair. Their knobs and branches shall so spring from it that the whole will form a single piece of pure beaten gold. You shall then make seven lamps for it and so set up the lamps that they give their light on the space in front of the menorah.

Action: The tabernacle is built from free-will offerings, each man allowing himself to be prompted by his heart. The result is a physical sign of God's presence among his people. Every family has their tent, and God has his tent, too. They are a nomadic people, so when they pick up and move, they roll up God's tent and he comes with them.

Acknowledge: Read the passage a second time. God has "pitched his tent" among the tents of the Israelites. Notice the thoughts, feelings, or desires that rise in your heart. How does it feel that God is traveling with his people? What would it feel like to be part of this nomadic nation?

Relate: Use your imagination to visit the tabernacle. Share with God whatever is on your heart.

Receive: Read the passage a third time. This time just receive whatever it is that God wants to give you.

Respond: The Lord cherishes your presence among his people. It wouldn't be the same without you. Cherish his presence with you for a few minutes before moving on.

SUGGESTIONS FOR JOURNALING

1. I was struck by …
2. My strongest thought, feeling, or desire was …
3. God wanted me to know that …
4. In what way(s) does God continue to make his presence visible to his people?
5. Moses is up the mountain from chapters 24 to 31. Chapter 32 tells us that the people got sick of waiting for him to come back down the mountain and they make for themselves a golden calf. What does this say about the human heart?

After you've journaled, close with a brief conversation giving thanks to God for his living presence in your prayer time today. Then pray an Our Father.

Wednesday of the Third Week in Ordinary Time

Preparation: *Come, Holy Spirit, enlighten the eyes of my heart.* Be present to the God who is always present to you. Call to mind his loving care for you and spend the first minute of your prayer just resting in the free, unearned gift of loving and being loved. Let gratitude rise in your heart.

Set the Scene: Ask God in your own words for the grace to understand yourself as a "Temple of the Holy Spirit." Now that the Israelites have taken possession of the promised land, it is time to build a permanent home for the Ark of the Covenant. Solomon, the son of King David, has finally completed the building of a temple. It is time for the dedication sacrifices. Use your imagination to picture the scene.

1 KINGS 8:1–13

Then Solomon assembled the elders of Israel and all the heads of the tribes, the princes in the ancestral houses of the Israelites. They came to King Solomon in Jerusalem, to bring up the ark of the LORD's covenant from the city of David (which is Zion). All the people of Israel assembled before King Solomon during the festival in the month of Ethanim (the seventh month). When all the elders of Israel had arrived, the priests took up the ark; and they brought up the ark of the LORD and the tent of meeting with all the sacred vessels that were in the tent. The priests and Levites brought them up. King Solomon and the entire community of Israel, gathered for the occasion before the ark, sacrificed sheep and oxen too many to number or count. The priests brought the ark of the covenant of the LORD to its place, the inner sanctuary of the house, the holy of holies, beneath the wings of the cherubim. The cherubim had their wings spread out over the place of the ark, sheltering the ark and its poles from above. The poles were so long that their ends could be seen from the holy place in front of the inner sanctuary. They cannot be seen from outside, but they remain there to this day. There was nothing in the ark but the two stone tablets which Moses had put there at Horeb, when the LORD made a covenant with the Israelites after they went forth from the land of Egypt. When the priests left the holy place, the cloud filled the house of the LORD so that the priests could no longer minister because of the cloud, since the glory of the LORD had filled the house of the LORD. Then Solomon said,

> *"The LORD intends to dwell in the dark cloud;*
> *I have indeed built you a princely house,*
> *the base for your enthronement forever."*

Action: They move the Ark into the Holy of Holies, and God makes his presence known in a dark cloud. The same cloud that indicated God's presence on Mount Sinai now takes up residence in the house that Solomon built for him. The Temple mountain is a holy mountain, a place where the people can connect with their God. How does Solomon feel at this visible sign? What do the priests feel? What does this say to the people?

Acknowledge: Read the passage a second time. Notice what thoughts come to your mind or what feelings arise in your heart.

Relate: There may not be a cloud of glory in your prayer space, but God is with you nonetheless. Speak to him. Share with him what is on your heart.

Receive: Read the passage a third time. Receive whatever is in God's heart for you. How does God desire to dwell with you today?

Respond: Respond to whatever God has given you. You, too, are a worthy dwelling for the Lord. Let him dwell within you for a few minutes before you move on.

SUGGESTIONS FOR JOURNALING
1. I was very moved by …
2. I understand the temple in a new way …
3. I know that God is with me because …
4. The presence of God is like …
5. I felt that God was calling me to …

After you've journaled, close with a brief conversation giving thanks to God for your prayer experience. Then pray an Our Father.

January 30 — Thursday
Thursday of the Third Week in Ordinary Time

Preparation: *Come, Holy Spirit, enlighten the eyes of my heart.* Be present to the God who is always present to you. Call to mind his loving care for you and spend the first minute of your prayer just resting in the free, unearned gift of loving and being loved. Let gratitude rise in your heart.

Lectio: Ask God in your own words for the grace to understand what it means to be a "Temple of the Holy Spirit." The author of the Letter to the Hebrews makes the case that Jesus is the High Priest and he offered the one perfect sacrifice, which was his own life. He argues that the Temple in Jerusalem and all the animal sacrifices were merely a preparation for this perfect sacrifice. Read the passage below slowly and prayerfully.

HEBREWS 9:11–14, 24–28

But when Christ came as high priest of the good things that have come to be, passing through the greater and more perfect tabernacle not made by hands, that is, not belonging to this creation, he entered once for all into the sanctuary, not with the blood of goats and calves but with his own blood, thus obtaining eternal redemption. For if the blood of goats and bulls and the sprinkling of a heifer's ashes can sanctify those who are defiled so that their flesh is cleansed, how much more will the blood of Christ, who through the eternal spirit offered himself unblemished to God, cleanse our consciences from dead works to worship the living God.

For Christ did not enter into a sanctuary made by hands, a copy of the true one, but heaven itself, that he might now appear before God on our behalf. Not that he might offer himself repeatedly, as the high priest enters each year into the sanctuary with blood that is not his own; if that were so, he would have had to suffer repeatedly from the foundation of the world. But now once for all he has appeared at the end of the ages to take away sin by his sacrifice. Just as it is appointed that human beings die once, and after this the judgment, so also Christ, offered once to take away the sins of many, will appear a second time, not to take away sin but to bring salvation to those who eagerly await him.

Meditatio: How is it that every sin that ever was, or ever will be, could have been forgiven in this one perfect sacrifice of Jesus Christ? This is the load he carried on the road to Calvary. We join in his priesthood whenever we join our sacrifices to his and when we participate in the sacrifice of Holy Mass. Do you eagerly await his Second Coming?

Oratio: Read the passage a second time. Do we not owe Jesus an incredible debt of gratitude? What are the best ways to say thank you? Picture Jesus and speak to him from your heart.

Contemplatio: Read the passage a third time. This time receive whatever Jesus wants to give you. Then spend a few minutes in grateful contemplation of this "love beyond measure" before moving on.

SUGGESTIONS FOR JOURNALING
1. The forgiveness of sins means to me …
2. I more fully appreciate the gift of …
3. Jesus wanted me to know …
4. I ended prayer with a deeper gratitude and appreciation for …
5. I can say thank you by …

After you've journaled, close with a brief conversation giving thanks to God for your experience of grace and mercy today. Then pray an Our Father.

January 31 — Friday
Friday of the Third Week in Ordinary Time

ST. JOHN BOSCO

His father died when he was two years old. His mother raised him and his two older brothers. Despite his family's poverty, his mother always found something to share with the homeless and the needy who came begging at their door. As a young boy, he watched a circus performance. He was so impressed that he learned how to do tricks himself. One Sunday afternoon he put on a show for the neighborhood kids, which won widespread applause. He then recited the homily he had heard earlier in the day and ended the show by inviting his audience to pray with him. He would go on to be ordained a priest and spend much of his life serving street children, attracting their attention with games and fun and then inviting them to learn how to live good, useful, and virtuous lives. He ultimately founded a religious order, the Salesian Society (named after St. Francis de Sales), to continue his work. He died in 1888.

Preparation: *Come, Holy Spirit, enlighten the eyes of my heart.* Be present to the God who is always present to you. Call to mind his loving care for you and spend the first minute of your prayer just resting in the free, unearned gift of loving and being loved. Let gratitude rise in your heart.

Set the Scene: Ask God in your own words for the grace to understand the final destination for we who are "Temples of the Holy Spirit." We get to our last day of meditating and there is no more Temple. There is no longer a need to go to a special place to worship God because he, himself, is always present to the redeemed in heaven. Read the Scripture passage and try to use your imagination to picture what this will be like.

REVELATION 21:1–4, 22–27

Then I saw a new heaven and a new earth. The former heaven and the former earth had passed away, and the sea was no more. I also saw the holy city, a new Jerusalem, coming down out of heaven from God, prepared as a bride adorned for her husband. I heard a loud voice from the throne saying, "Behold, God's dwelling is with the human race. He will dwell with them and they will be his people and God himself will always be with them [as their God]. He will wipe every tear from their eyes, and there shall be no more death or mourning, wailing or pain, [for] the old order has passed away."

I saw no temple in the city, for its temple is the Lord God almighty and the Lamb. The city had no need of sun or moon to shine on it, for the glory of God gave it light, and its lamp was the Lamb. The nations will walk by its light, and to it the kings of the earth will bring their treasure. During the day its gates will never be shut, and there will be no night there. The treasure and wealth of the nations will be brought there, but nothing unclean will enter it, nor any[one] who does abominable things or tells lies. Only those will enter whose names are written in the Lamb's book of life.

Action: Jerusalem is the archetype of the "Holy City," a place where God's people live in harmony with their God. The physical city here on earth is only an analogy pointing to the true and eternal city. No one lies or does evil things in this city. Therefore, liars must give up lying if they wish to enter or remain forever outside. God desires all to enter, but the choice is up to us if we accept the invitation and allow God to make us worthy to dwell in love with him and the holy ones. How does God feel? How do the redeemed feel?

Acknowledge: Read the passage a second time. What comes to mind? How does the passage make you feel? What fears or desires surface for you?

Relate: Speak to God, and to the Lamb.

Receive: Read the passage a third time, or the part that most moved you on the previous readings. What is on God's heart for you?

Respond: Answer God, then rest with the one who is excited to be with you forever in the eternal kingdom. Spend a few minutes savoring God's love for you before moving on.

SUGGESTIONS FOR JOURNALING

1. What I noticed about heaven was …
2. The thing that bothered me or made me fearful was …
3. I noticed a deep desire for …
4. God wanted me to know …
5. I ended prayer wanting to …

After you've journaled, close with a brief conversation giving thanks to God for not only wanting to be with you forever, but for being with you right now in your prayer experience. Then pray an Our Father.

February 1 — Saturday

Saturday of the Third Week in Ordinary Time

REVIEW

Preparation: *Come, Holy Spirit, enlighten the eyes of my heart.* Call to mind God's loving care for you and spend the first minute of your prayer just resting in the free, unearned gift of loving and being loved. Let gratitude rise in your heart.

Grace of the Day: What is the desire of your heart? Try to notice what you most deeply desire. Then share it with God in your own words, being confident that he loves you and wants to give you every blessing.

Week in Review: Flip back through your past week's journal entries. As you do, notice what emerged in the conversation. Here are some questions to help you:

1. Where did I notice God, and what was he doing or saying?
2. How did I respond to what God was doing?
3. I felt God's love most strongly when …
4. I found myself struggling with …
5. I'm grateful for …
6. This past week, my strongest sense, image, moment, or experience of God's loving presence was …

_____

_____

_____

_____

_____

_____

_____

_____

_____

_____

_____

_____

_____

_____

_____

_____

_____

_____

Conclude by conversing with God about your week. **Acknowledge** what you have been experiencing. **Relate** it to him. **Receive** what he wants to give you. **Respond** to him. Then savor that image of God's loving presence and rest there for a minute or two. Close with an Our Father.

Week Ten

He Has Called You Out of Darkness into His Own Wonderful Light

This year we have the joy of celebrating the feast of the Presentation on a Sunday. This feast commemorates the day that Mary and Joseph brought the baby Jesus to the Temple (see Lk 2:22–40). The law of Moses required the purification of a mother forty days after the birth of a male child (Lv 12:1–8). It also stipulated that the firstborn belonged to the priests. A firstborn cow, sheep, or goat would be sacrificed to God, but not a child. The firstborn son was instead ransomed by a payment of money (Ex 13:11–16; Nm 18:13–16). This is a reference to the tenth plague in Egypt, the death of the firstborn, and perhaps the sacrifice of Isaac (Gn 22:2–8). Mary and Joseph have, then, two reasons to come to the Temple forty days after the birth of Jesus.

Saint Luke loves the Temple (his Gospel begins and ends in the Temple, and his symbol is the ox, a sacrificial animal). The way that he writes about this moment, Jesus isn't being redeemed but rather *presented*. The unseen God has been worshiped here for centuries. Now God himself, in the Person of Jesus, is visiting his own Temple. He comes in the humble form of a little baby. However, his visit does not go unnoticed. Simeon and Anna have grown old waiting for God's promises to be fulfilled. And they have not been disappointed.

Simeon declares:

> Now, Master, you may let your servant go
>   in peace, according to your word,
> for my eyes have seen your salvation,
>   which you prepared in sight of all the peoples,
> a light for revelation to the Gentiles,
>   and glory for your people Israel. (Luke 2:29–32)

Remember how back at the beginning of Advent we were told to watch? These two old people are the only ones still watching. And they are rewarded with a vision of the Savior who is Christ and Lord. Simeon and Anna perfectly symbolize what our *Oriens* pilgrimage is all about. Faith in God has opened the eyes of their hearts to see God's presence and action in apparently ordinary moments. They recognize Jesus, the Light of the World, and they begin to glow with his divine light.

The feast of the Presentation also goes by the old English name Candlemas. A prominent feature of our liturgical celebration is the blessing of candles. The candles remind us of the Advent wreath and how our light grew brighter as the world grew darker. We then go forth with lighted candles to meet our Lord, processing from another location into the church building. The feast itself is a pilgrimage! The procession with lit candles reminds us of the blessing and procession of palms that will happen on Palm Sunday. The lit candles also foreshadow the Easter Vigil, when we celebrate Jesus rising from the darkness of death to shed his peaceful light on humanity.

We spent roughly four weeks of Advent preparing for Christ. Now we have spent forty days celebrating Christmas. In a similar way, we will soon begin our Lenten fast of forty days, followed by fifty days of Easter feasting. The feast of Candlemas calls us back to Christmas and forward to Easter.

Grace of the Week: My prayer for every pilgrim is that your eyes have been enlightened to see God's presence and action more clearly in your everyday life. I pray that Christmastime has lit your heart on fire and that you, too, have begun to glow more brightly with the warmth of divine love. Keep tending your candle! Keep burning and glowing with the light of faith. Carry that light to the dark corners of the world, that the light of God's love will begin to spread to every heart and fill every home.

February 2 — Sunday
Feast of the Presentation of the Lord

"The *presentation of Jesus in the temple* shows him to be the firstborn Son who belongs to the Lord. With Simeon and Anna, all Israel awaits its *encounter* with the Savior — the name given to this event in the Byzantine tradition. Jesus is recognized as the long-expected Messiah, the 'light to the nations' and the 'glory of Israel,' but also 'a sign that is spoken against.' The sword of sorrow predicted for Mary announces Christ's perfect and unique oblation on the cross that will impart the salvation God had 'prepared in the presence of all peoples'" (*Catechism of the Catholic Church*, 529).

Preparation: *Come, Holy Spirit, enlighten the eyes of my heart.* Be present to the God who is always present to you. Call to mind his loving care for you and spend the first minute of your prayer just resting in the free, unearned gift of loving and being loved. Let gratitude rise in your heart.

Set the Scene: Ask God for the grace to carry his light to the dark corners of the world, that the light of God's love will begin to spread to every heart and fill every home. The Temple in Jerusalem is the largest and most impressive building that most Jews have ever seen. But soon it will all be destroyed, replaced by the one perfect sacrifice and the New Covenant in the blood of Jesus. In this humble moment, God is entering his Temple. Read the passage and picture the enormous Temple, the elderly couple, and the babe who is God from God and Light from Light.

LUKE 2:22–40 (LECTIONARY)
When the days were completed for their purification according to the law of Moses, they took him up to Jerusalem to present him to the Lord, just as it is written in the law of the Lord, Every male that opens the womb shall be consecrated to the Lord, *and to offer the sacrifice of* a pair of turtledoves or two young pigeons, *in accordance*

290 *February 2 — Sunday*

with the dictate in the law of the Lord.

Now there was a man in Jerusalem whose name was Simeon. This man was righteous and devout, awaiting the consolation of Israel, and the Holy Spirit was upon him. It had been revealed to him by the Holy Spirit that he should not see death before he had seen the Christ of the Lord. He came in the Spirit into the temple; and when the parents brought in the child Jesus to perform the custom of the law in regard to him, he took him into his arms and blessed God, saying:

> "Now, Master, you may let your servant go
> in peace, according to your word,
> for my eyes have seen your salvation,
> which you prepared in sight of all the peoples,
> a light for revelation to the Gentiles,
> and glory for your people Israel."

The child's father and mother were amazed at what was said about him; and Simeon blessed them and said to Mary his mother, "Behold, this child is destined for the fall and rise of many in Israel, and to be a sign that will be contradicted — and you yourself a sword will pierce — so that the thoughts of many hearts may be revealed." There was also a prophetess, Anna, the daughter of Phanuel, of the tribe of Asher. She was advanced in years, having lived seven years with her husband after her marriage, and then as a widow until she was eighty-four. She never left the temple, but worshiped night and day with fasting and prayer. And coming forward at that very time, she gave thanks to God and spoke about the child to all who were awaiting the redemption of Jerusalem.

When they had fulfilled all the prescriptions of the law of the Lord, they returned to Galilee, to their own town of Nazareth. The child grew and became strong, filled with wisdom; and the favor of God was upon him.

Action: The rest of the people are going about their business never realizing the amazing thing that is happening. Simeon and Anna see more because they see with the eyes of faith. Notice what is going on in their hearts. What does your faith enable you to see in this scene? Use your imagination.

Acknowledge: Read the passage a second time. Notice what part speaks to you. What is going on inside of you? How does your heart leap for joy? What do you feel and experience? Ask Mary to let you hold her child.

Relate: Speak to the Christ Child, heart to heart. Invite him into your heart.

Receive: Read the passage again, but this time just focus on the part that speaks to you. Open your heart to receive all that God wants to give you.

Respond: Jesus lives in the heart of every believer. Welcome him into your heart. Let your heart enter into a deeper communion with the Sacred Heart, the Word-made-Flesh. Let him cast out your darkness and fill you with his pure light.

SUGGESTIONS FOR JOURNALING

1. I was surprised by …
2. The part that most spoke to me was …
3. The greatest gift God has given me on this pilgrimage was …
4. In exchange, I found God wanting me to give him …
5. I ended prayer wanting …

After you've journaled, close with a brief conversation giving thanks to God for being the light of your life. Then pray an Our Father.

The Presentation of the Lord (Candlemas)

AT THE MASS

The people gather in the chapel or other suitable place outside the church where the Mass will be celebrated. They carry unlighted candles. The priest and his ministers wear white vestments. While the candles are being lighted, this canticle may be sung: *The Lord will come with mighty power, and give light to the eyes of all who serve him, alleluia.* Then the priest introduces the Mass:

Dear brothers and sisters, forty days have passed since we celebrated the joyful feast of the Nativity of the Lord. Today is the blessed day when Jesus was presented in the Temple by Mary and Joseph. Outwardly he was fulfilling the Law, but in reality he was coming to meet his believing people. Prompted by the Holy Spirit, Simeon and Anna came to the Temple. Enlightened by the same Spirit, they recognized the Lord and confessed him with exultation. So let us also, gathered together by the Holy Spirit, proceed to the house of God to encounter Christ. There we shall find him and recognize him in the breaking of the bread, until he comes again, revealed in glory.

Then he blesses the candles:

Let us pray. O God, source and origin of all light, who on this day showed to the just man Simeon the Light for revelation to the Gentiles, we humbly ask that, in answer to your people's prayers, you may be pleased to sanctify with your blessing ✠ these candles, which we are eager to carry in praise of your name, so that, treading the path of virtue, we may reach that light which never fails. Through Christ our Lord. Amen.

Let us go forth in peace.

The people respond: In the name of Christ. Amen.

From the Roman Missal, third typical edition, February 2

Once a Pilgrim,
Always a Pilgrim

Pilgrimages always seem to end abruptly. You strive to reach your destination, you struggle on the road, it seems as though you'll never get there. Then you realize it's the final day, the final miles, and the place of pilgrimage is just over the next hill! You have made it to your destination. You bask in the feeling of success, promise to stay in touch with your fellow pilgrims, and struggle to explain to your family what has happened to you.

Then it is back to your old life. But the old life looks different now; the journey has changed you. You see yourself, God, and the world around you in a different light. Hopefully you too have become a light. Christmas time has lit your heart with the warmth and light of God's love. Keep tending your candle! Keep burning and glowing with the light of faith. Carry that light to the dark corners of the world so that the light of God's love will spread to every heart and home.

REVIEW OF REVIEWS
When you have a little time, flip back to the very first day of your pilgrimage, Sunday, December 1, and look at how it all began. Then take a journey through the eight Saturday review days. Notice what was coming up. Reflect on where you have been and how God has been with you on the journey. Notice how the journey has changed you.

SUGGESTIONS FOR JOURNALING
1. How did God meet me on the road?
2. There's so much! But the part that most spoke to me was ...
3. God was telling me that ...
4. I was able to let go of ...
5. The deepest desire that has emerged in my heart is ...
6. The greatest gift(s) God has given me on this pilgrimage is ...
7. In exchange, I found God asking me to give him the gift ...
8. If I was going to try and put into words my newfound relationship with God, I would describe it as ...

9. My strongest thought, image, or experience of God's love has been …

Acknowledge what the pilgrimage meant to you. **Relate** it to God. **Receive** what he wants to give you. **Respond** to him. Then savor God's loving presence and rest there for a minute or two. Close with an Our Father.

The Journey Continues

Keep walking! Our pilgrimage is never done until we *come to the end of our pilgrimage and enter the presence of God*. Here are some suggestions for you to continue the journey:

- Buy a journal. At the end of each day, answer four questions: 1) What blessings did I experience today? 2) What burden or challenge did I face? 3) Where did I see Jesus today? 4) Who was I Jesus to today? Use the ARRR prayer form (on page 247) to pray with your daily experiences and journal the fruits of your prayer.
- On the following pages, I give you outlines for four different forms of prayer. You might want to tear out those pages and keep them with your journal.
- Start praying with the daily Scripture readings. You can find each day's readings at usccb.org/bible/readings/. Depending on the reading, you can use *lectio divina* or Imaginative Prayer for your prayer each day (see the Prayer Outlines on pages 243 and 245).
- Subscribe to a monthly missal. I have used *Magnificat* for years, and I find it very helpful. It includes prayer for morning and evening, the daily readings, and some reflections and additional prayers. There are many other monthly missals to choose from and all of them will help you pray daily.
- Another great journal option is *Every Sacred Sunday*, which has readings and journal space for Sundays and holy days. Check it out at everysacredsunday.com.
- Need more help journaling? Check out the Monk Manual at monkmanual.com. This resource provides reflection space and prompts for you on a daily, weekly, and monthly basis. It helps you live life with more reflection and purpose.
- Subscribe to my homily podcast. Learn more at

PilgrimPriest.us/podcast.

- OSV has a number of Bible study resources. Browse their offerings at www.osvcatholicbookstore.com/product-category/bibles-bible-studies. Consider not only participating in a Bible study, but actually leading one at your local church or in your home.
- Lent is coming up soon. Start reflecting and praying about a theme for Lent and how to live Lent more intentionally.
- Consider making a real, honest-to-goodness walking pilgrimage. My diocese hosts the Walk to Mary every year, a one-day walking pilgrimage. Learn more at walktomary.com. Check out my website, PilgrimPriest.us, for the article "A Step-by-Step Guide to Walking Pilgrimages."

Prayer Outlines

LECTIO DIVINA

Lectio divina can be used with any passage from Scripture. The key is to use Scripture as a conversation starter for a deep, personal conversation with the God who inspired it. Don't rush each step; let them naturally unfold. Remember that the goal is spending quality time with the God who loves you. As you Read, Think, Talk, and Listen, you will learn to spend time with God like an old friend.

Preparation: *Come, Holy Spirit, enlighten the eyes of my heart.* Be present to the God who is always present to you. Call to mind his loving care for you and spend the first minute of your prayer just resting in the free, unearned gift of loving and being loved. Let gratitude rise in your heart.

Lectio: Listen to the desire of your heart, then ask God for whatever it is you desire to receive in today's prayer time. Read the passage through, slowly and prayerfully.

Meditatio: Turn the passage over in your mind. The ancients compared meditation to a cow chewing its cud. What was the cultural context? What did the author mean? Perhaps a particular word, phrase, or idea speaks to you. Perhaps it connects to a previous meditation or another Scripture passage. What are your feelings as you read the passage?

Oratio: Read the passage a second time. Prayer must be a conversation between persons. Turn to God and begin a conversation with him. Speak to him what is on your heart — your thoughts, feelings, fears, and desires.

Contemplatio: Read the passage a third time. Now just receive what is on God's heart — his thoughts, feelings, and desires. Spend some time receiving God's love and resting in it. Prayer is experiencing how our Father looks at us with love. Holiness is learning to live in his long, loving gaze every moment of our life.

SUGGESTIONS FOR JOURNALING

Journaling isn't an essential part of the prayer, but I find that it helps me to deepen the experience when I put into words what was happening in the prayer time. You might find questions like these helpful, or you might make your own list of journal questions:

1. The part that most spoke to me was ...
2. What I brought to the Lord was ...
3. God gave me ...
4. I received a new insight, understanding, or sense of myself ...
5. Apply something from the passage to your own life.(For example, a passage about John the Baptist: Who pointed out Jesus to me? When did I point out Jesus to another person, or what virtue of John the Baptist do I feel called to imitate?)

After you've journaled, close with a brief conversation giving thanks to God for the prayer time together. End with an Our Father or another favorite prayer.

IMAGINATIVE PRAYER

Imaginative prayer helps us disconnect from this present moment in order to connect you with the deep reality of God's loving, invisible presence with you right now. The goal is not to build great imaginary castles in the air. You want to look into the Bible and through it encounter the God who was present in the moment when the biblical passage was written and is present here with you today. The imagination helps to break the ice and start the conversation as you spend quality time with God. It works best with Scriptures that have a lot of visual description or action to them.

Preparation: *Come, Holy Spirit, enlighten the eyes of my heart.* Be present to the God who is always present to you. Call to mind his loving care for you and spend the first minute of your prayer just resting in the free, unearned gift of loving and being loved. Let gratitude rise in your heart.

Set the Scene: Listen to the desire of your heart, then ask God for whatever it is that you desire to receive in today's prayer time. Read the passage through and picture the scene in your mind. Choose the time of day and the scenery. Populate it with people dressed in period clothes. (Alternatively, you can picture the scene happening in your own city or neighborhood.)

Action: Play the scene forward in your mind. Notice how the participants react and what they are thinking and feeling. Notice where Jesus is and what he is doing. (You can also notice Mary, God the Father, the Holy Spirit, etc.) Place yourself in the scene.

Acknowledge: Read the passage a second time. What does this passage stir up in your mind and heart? Pay attention to your thoughts, feelings, and desires. Don't worry if they are "correct," just notice them without any judgment.

Relate: As the scene is finished, spend some time in conversation with

Jesus. You can walk with him, sit with him in the scene, or just be aware of his presence in your prayer space. Share your thoughts, feelings, desires, and fears, honestly and openly.

Receive: Read the passage a third time. How does God respond to what you have shared? What is in God's heart for you? Receiving isn't meant to be hard work. It is about relaxing into God's loving presence, focusing on him, and noticing what word, Scripture passage, feeling, or reminder might come.

Respond: This is a chance to deepen the conversation. Ask a question about what God seems to be saying or just say thank you. And like good friends, let yourself just enjoy God's company for a little while.

SUGGESTIONS FOR JOURNALING

1. Something in my life that connected with the story was …
2. As the scene played out, what struck me was …
3. I talked to Jesus about …
4. I sensed that he wanted me to know, or to give me, or remind me …
5. I left prayer with a new insight, understanding, or a call to a new way of thinking or acting …

After you've journaled, close with a brief conversation giving thanks to God for your prayer experience. Then pray an Our Father or another favorite prayer.

Relational Prayer (ARRR)

Relational prayer is a great way of praying with the experiences of every-day life. No matter what kinds of struggles or challenges you are facing, you can always pause and take a moment to give them to God. Here's how you do it:

Preparation: *Come, Holy Spirit, enlighten the eyes of my heart.* Be present to the God who is always present to you. Call to mind his loving care for you and spend the first minute of your prayer just resting in the free, unearned gift of loving and being loved. Let gratitude rise in your heart.

Acknowledge: Notice what is going on inside of you — your thoughts, feelings, and desires. Helpful statements include, "When he did/said/act-ed that way, it made me feel _____." If you are feeling too angry to concen-trate, pray the name of Jesus a few times and stick with the preparation period until you notice his peaceful presence. With anger in particular, it is helpful to try and notice what you were thinking and feeling just before you got angry. That can be a clue to where the anger came from, and what God might want you to share with him.

Relate: Share with the Lord what is going on inside of you. Be honest with God. Sometimes we are mad at God himself because he appears to be ruining our lives or ignoring our prayers. You can get mad at God. Tell him how you feel, even if it includes inappropriate words. It's really important that we be completely honest. Do not try and ask God to give you something or do something at this stage. Just tell him what is going on with you.

Receive: Now we shift our attention from us and our problems to God. This is where I often got stuck when I was learning this prayer form. Picture this scene: I'm struggling with something. A good friend comes and stands next to me. I point out the problem, tell him everything, and he listens patiently. God and I are looking at my problem together. Now, I turn to focus on my friend. What is in his heart for me? How does he look at me? It's his turn to talk. Sometimes it's just knowing that he cares, a feeling of peace, or that I am not alone in my problem. Sometimes it might be a Scripture passage or a few words to put me in my place or add perspective. Like with any good friend, it may not be exactly what I want to hear, but it will be what I need to hear.

Respond: If what he just gave you is hard to receive, tell him so. If it comforts you, thank him. Even if you don't get anything at this time, you can be confident that God will answer you when he is ready and will give you what you really need. So keep your eyes and ears open in case he has more to say or give you later.

Sharing your burdens with God makes them melt like snow in the sunshine. It's almost like magic, but better. We call it "grace." Practice this prayer time with the experiences of your everyday life.

SUGGESTIONS FOR JOURNALING

1. My strongest thought, feeling, or emotion was …
2. I needed to share with God that …
3. God wanted me to know …
4. In the course of my prayer time, I realized that …
5. I ended prayer with a new way of thinking, acting, responding, or believing …
6. I feel called by God to …

Feel free to journal whatever from the above struck you. Then spend a few minutes thanking God for the quality time together and end with an Our Father or another favorite prayer.

The Saturday Review

I like to keep an old canning jar as a "Gratitude Jar." I start at New Year's, and each Saturday I write on a slip of paper the one thing that I am most grateful for that week and add it to the jar. At the end of the year, I dump out the jar and review my blessings. If you're interested in adopting this practice for yourself, a Saturday review like those we did throughout the *Oriens* pilgrimage can help fill your jar.

Preparation: *Come, Holy Spirit, enlighten the eyes of my heart.* Call to mind God's loving care for you and spend the first minute of your prayer just resting in the free, unearned gift of loving and being loved. Let gratitude rise in your heart.

Grace of the Day: What is the desire of your heart? Try to notice what you must deeply desire. Then share it with God in your own words, being confident that he loves you and wants to give you every blessing.

Week in Review: Flip back through your past week's journal entries. As you do, notice what emerged in the conversation. Here are some questions to help you:

Preparation: *Come, Holy Spirit, enlighten the eyes of my heart.* Call to mind his loving care for you and spend the first minute of your prayer just resting in the free, unearned gift of loving and being loved. Let gratitude rise in your heart.

1. My biggest blessing in the past week was …
2. My biggest challenge was …
3. Where did I notice God, and what was he doing or saying?
4. How did I respond to what God was doing?
5. I felt God's love most strongly when …
6. I'm grateful for …
7. This past week, my strongest sense, image, moment, or experience of God's loving presence was …

Conclude by conversing with God about your week. **Acknowledge** what you have been experiencing. **Relate** it to him. **Receive** what he wants to give you. **Respond** to him. Then savor that image of God's loving presence and rest there for a minute or two. Close with a Glory Be.

Acknowledgments

Thank you to Our Lady, Queen of Heaven, who appeared in Champion, Wisconsin, in 1859. Thank you to the Shrine of Our Lady of Good Help for welcoming pilgrims as a place of prayer, peace, and hospitality.

I am grateful to Tim, my first partner on pilgrimage, and all my fellow walking pilgrims through the years. Your companionship has richly blessed and encouraged me.

To Father Paul, Father Tom, Father Ryan, Father Michael, and my priestly fraternity group, Father Looney, and the priests and people of the Diocese of Green Bay.

Thank you to the awesome staff and loving parish families of St. John the Evangelist, Saints Mary and Hyacinth, Saint Wenceslaus, and Saints James and Stanislaus parishes.

Thank you to the Institute for Priestly Formation for my training as a spiritual director. This book is a fruit of their ministry, which is why I am donating my royalties to support their work. Learn more at www .priestlyformation.org.

Thank you to my loving family, and especially my parents, Jim and Marion, who often tell me that they love me and are proud of me.

I am grateful to Mary Beth Giltner and the staff of OSV Books for making this book happen for the fifth year in a row.

And to you, my fellow *Oriens* pilgrim. I wrote this book for you. I hope that we meet some day, in this life or the next. The best is yet to come!

About the Author

Fr. Joel Sember was ordained a priest in 2007 for the Diocese of Green Bay, Wisconsin. He has extensive experience as a parish priest and two years of service in campus ministry. He made a thirty-day Ignatian silent retreat and later completed the Spiritual Direction Training Program through the Institute for Priestly Formation in Omaha, Nebraska. He holds a bachelor's in philosophy and catholic studies from the University of St. Thomas, a bachelor's in sacred theology from the Pontifical Gregorian University, and a license in sacred theology from the Pontifical University Santa Croce in Rome. He has completed a dozen walking pilgrimages. He currently serves as pastor of four parishes in rural northeastern Wisconsin. Between ministry and parish meetings, he rides a motorcycle and paddles a kayak around great Wisconsin lakes. You can listen to his homily podcast every Sunday at PilgrimPriest.us.